Computer Support for Successful Project Management

Computer Support for Successful Project Management

Using MS Project 2016 with Information Technology Projects

Ulhas M. Samant

BEP BUSINESS EXPERT PRESS

Computer Support for Successful Project Management: Using MS Project 2016 with Information Technology Projects

First published in 2018 by
Business Expert Press, LLC
222 East 46th Street, New York, NY 10017
www.businessexpertpress.com

ISBN-13: 978-1-60649-750-0 (paperback)
ISBN-13: 978-1-60649-751-7 (e-book)

Business Expert Press Information Systems Collection

Collection ISSN: 2156-6577 (print)
Collection ISSN: 2156-6593 (electronic)

Cover and interior design by Exeter Premedia Services Private Ltd., Chennai, India

First edition: 2018

10 9 8 7 6 5 4 3 2 1

Printed in the United States of America.

The book is dedicated to my father, late Mr. Muralidhar V Samant,
who encouraged to pursue my dreams

Abstract

In the recent past, computer programs have been used extensively to manage Information Technology projects. It has become almost mandatory for software development managers and students of Information Technology to learn how to use computer software to manage projects using computer software.

Computer Support for Successful Project Management: Using MS Project 2016 with Information Technology Projects is a book intended to help Information Technology management professionals and students, in using popular software MS-Project. Although there are many books on MS-Project, there are very few that cover the subject from the Information Technology managers' perspective. This book uses guided examples from the Information Technology sector. Most of the relevant project management terminology, concepts, and key processes have also been discussed, based on the standards of the Project Management Institute. This book helps software development project managers to easily relate with the projects they execute in their day-to-day life.

The author has included advanced topics like earned value analysis and multiple project management. A discussion on Agile Methodology and how MS-Project facilitates Agile Project Management has been included in the book. You also learn how a tool like MS-Project can be used for processes related to risk, quality, and so on, in addition to meeting project objectives like scope, time, and cost. This book helps you to transform yourself from an Information Technology professional to an Information Technology project manager.

Keywords

agile, information technology, Microsoft Office Project, MS Project, Office Project, PMBOK, PMI, Project 2016, project management, project professional, scheduling software, software development, software project management

Contents

Acknowledgments

I would like to thank a few of the many who supported me while writing this book. I thank our technical reviewers, Mohamed Bedjaoui, an experienced teacher of project management, and Michael Wharton (of Wharton Computer Consulting) for their timely and valuable expertise. I am also thankful to Ravi Shankar Nadibail, an independent consultant from Mumbai, India, for checking the correctness of examples. I thank our executive acquisitions editor, Scott Isenberg, and his entire team of Business Expert Press (Momentum Press), for their outstanding work.

Introduction

About This Book

In recent years, Microsoft Project (MS-Project) has evolved as a powerful tool for creating and managing projects, across various domains. The Information Technology is a sector where timely delivery of projects is very important. It becomes all the more important to estimate the schedule and cost of projects properly and also track the projects. Although there are many books on using MS-Project for managing projects, very few of them discuss the functionality with examples from the Information Technology sector. *Computer Support for Successful Project Management: Using MS Project 2016 with Information Technology Projects* offers a comprehensive look at some of the key project management processes and also how engineers, practitioners from the Information Technology sector, can use features of MS-Project to their advantage.

This book starts with an introduction to Software Process Models and Project Management. Subsequently, the key project management processes related to project scope, time and cost management are discussed. Once the discussion about arriving at project schedule and cost concludes, it discusses about project monitoring. This book also deals with additional topics like managing multiple projects and using MS-Project in managing other project objectives like risk and quality. More importantly, the book discusses using MS-Project for Agile project management, though in brief.

In addition, this book includes several appendices. The appendices give you an introduction to Microsoft project, project server, and using MS Project with other office products.

Assumptions About You

This book assumes that you have experience in using MS Windows and also in using some MS Office applications like MS Excel. It also assumes that you have knowledge related to Information technology.

How to Use This Book

This book facilitates you to work with MS-Project Professional 2016 (and also with Project Standard). However, if you have not used it, it is better to go through Appendix-C, *A Quick Introduction to MS Project 2016*, to start with. If you have not undergone any formal project management training program, going through the first chapter (Chapter 1) helps you to understand project organizations and different knowledge areas of project management. Chapters 2 to 11 discuss using MS-Project to manage projects.

Appendix D discusses using MS-Project with other office products like Excel and PowerPoint. Chapters 2 to 11, Appendix C, and Appendix D can be roughly divided between two portions. The first portion is an explanatory part, which defines the core concept, and the second contains hands-on activity (enumerated procedure). Examples from the Information Technology sector have been used both for explaining the core concept and hands-on exercise. The hands-on activities are guided exercises and may require practice files. All the files are in the folder *Practice-files* and the folder can be downloaded from the web page:

http://businessexpertpress.com/books/computer-support
-for-successful-project-management-using-ms-project-2016-with
-information-technology-projects/

Please note that MS-Project program is not available on this website. You may have to purchase the same or download a trial version to use with the book.

The following table lists the practice files for hands-on exercises of this book.

Chapter number	Practice files
Chapter 1	No practice file
Chapter 2	Math Lib Original.mpp
Chapter 3	Porting-orginal.mpp
Chapter 4	ResourceAlloc1-orginal.mpp
Chapter 5	Math Lib-original.mpp Resource-Level-Start mpp
Chapter 6	Testing-project-with-resources -orginal.mpp

Chapter 7	enhancement-start.mpp web-site-improvement-start.mpp
Chapter 8	bank_app_desn_complete.mpp
Chapter 9	In *Dependency* folder two files hw-setup.mpp Testing-project.mpp In *Files-for-consolidation* folder two files AppDevelopment.mpp Testing-project.mpp
Chapter 10	AppDevelopment-start.mpp enhancement-start.mpp RiskRegister-Software-Project.xls
Chapter 11	Agile-project-management—Start
Appendix D	AppDevelopment.xls Project-Progress-Report.doc enhancement- complete.mpp

CHAPTER 1

Introduction to Information Technology Project Management

Objectives

1. Understand about the Software Process Model
2. Understand about the waterfall model and the Agile Development
3. Learn at Macro Level how MS-Project can help project managers

A Project is defined as a temporary endeavor undertaken to create a unique product, service, or result. For example, if you are creating a mobile app for a bank to enable the customers to do financial transactions, it is a project. If you are improving the performance of an enterprise grade information technology system, it is a project.

Project Phases and Phase-to-Phase Relationships

A project passes through a series of phases from the start to closure. The phases are time bound, and provide intermediate results (or deliverables). Broadly there can be three types of phase-to-phase relationships:

1. Sequential relationship, in which the project is divided into separate phases and each phase is carried out successively in sequence;
2. Overlapping relationship, in which phases may be overlapping;
3. Iterative relationship, which has been used extensively in the recent past for projects with rapidly changing requirements.

The Software Process and the Process Models

We did discuss about Project, Project Phases, and phase-to-phase relationships in earlier paragraphs. The sequence of phases for the entire lifetime of a product is described by a Process Model or a Product Life Cycle.
This covers everything from the initial commercial idea until the final
un-installation of a software product after its use. A Product Life Cycle is
longer than a Project Life Cycle. A Product Life Cycle can spawn many a
projects (Figure 1.1).

In addition to the phases, a Process Model will also give a picture of
the following:

- The **tasks** that have to be carried out in each of the phases or
  subphases, along with their sequence.
- The **role, responsibilities, and the essential skills** of the
  project team members or internal stake holders.
- The **work products or deliverables** that have to be generated
  or evolved in each of the activities. Besides the final product,
  there are usually several other items that have to be generated
  during the development of a product. For example, Software
  Architecture Document, Test reports.

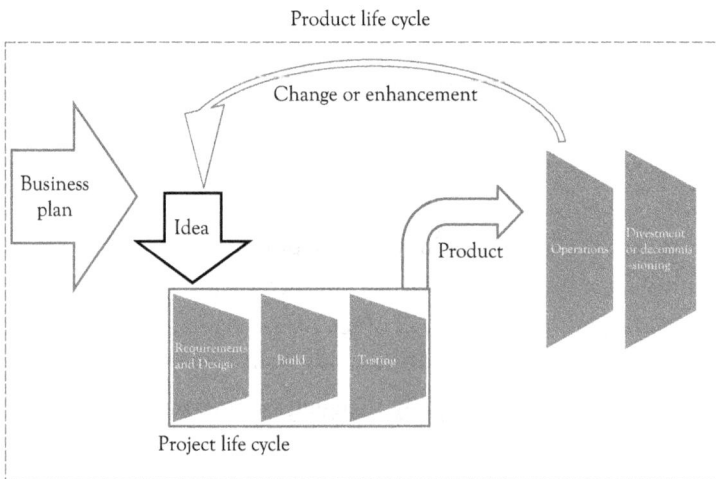

*Figure 1.1 Relation between Product Life Cycle and Project Life
Cycle*

Therefore, a Process Model provides a framework that guides planning and tracking of a project.

The Waterfall Model

The waterfall model is the first process model which was introduced and has been used in software engineering extensively. Initially computer programs used to be simple and primitive meeting a few specific requirements. As programs became bigger and complex, the need for a better requirements elicitation and thoughtful design and so on emerged. Programmers found it more and more difficult to keep an abstract of the program in their mind and transfer it directly into code. A separate and detailed testing phase performed by dedicated testers got evolved, to get the programs tested independently. The different phases of software engineering were identified and simply cascaded in each other (Figure 1.2), allowing for loops in case it was found in a subsequent phase that the previous phase was not done properly.

The phases of "The Waterfall Model" are:

Requirement Analysis and Definition: All requirements of the system which have to be developed are collected and analyzed during this phase. Like in other process models requirements are split up in functional requirements and constraints which the system has to fulfill. Requirements have to be collected by analyzing the needs of the end user(s) and other key stakeholders. Checking them for

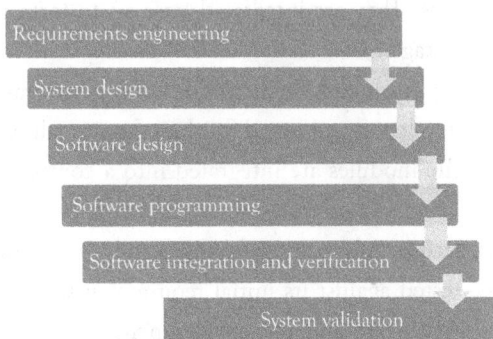

Figure 1.2 The Waterfall Model with different phases

validity and the possibility to implement them is also done at this stage. Requirements Specification Document is an outcome of this phase and it is used as an input for the next phase (that is system design) of the model.

System Design: This involves an architectural design which defines and describes the main blocks and components of the system, their interfaces and interactions. By this, the needed hardware is defined and the software is split up in its components. This phase generates a System Architecture Document. This not only serves as an input for the software design phase of the development, but also as an input for hardware design or selection activities. Usually in this phase various documents are generated, one for each discipline, so that the software usually will receive a software architecture document.

Software Design: The software design will break main blocks further down into code modules. The interfaces and interactions of the modules are described, as well as their functional contents. As an outcome, Software Design gets documented and forms base for the implementation work.

Coding: Actual coding is started. The system is first developed in smaller portions called units or modules. They are able to stand alone from a functional aspect and can be tested for the same. Each unit is developed independently and can be tested for its functionality. This is the so-called Unit Testing. It simply verifies if the modules or units to check if they meet their specifications. This involves not only functional tests at the interfaces of the modules, but also more detailed tests which consider the inner structure of the software modules. They are integrated later on to form the complete software package.

Software Integration and Verification: During integration the units which are developed and tested for their functionalities are brought together. The modules are integrated into a complete system and tested to check if all modules put together operate as expected.

System Validation: After successful integration, the complete system has to be tested against its initial requirements. This will include the actual hardware and the environment, whereas the previous integration and testing phase may still be performed in a different environment or on a test bench.

The system is delivered to the customer or the end user and will be used the first time by him. Not only the customers (or the end users) will check if the requirements were implemented as expected, but they will also validate if the correct requirements have been set up in the beginning. In case there are changes necessary, it has to be fixed to make the system usable or to make it comply with the customer wishes. In most of the "Waterfall Model" descriptions, this phase is extended to a never-ending phase of "Operations and Maintenance." All the problems which were not captured during the previous phases will be solved in this last phase. The Waterfall Model has several weaknesses. The prominent ones are:

- It is required to elicit all the requirements in the initial phase itself. However, in actual practice, only a part of the requirements is known at the beginning.
- Iterations are only meant to happen within the same phase or at best from the start of the subsequent phase back to the previous phase. This develops the tendency to patch problems with insufficient fixing of problems than solving root causes.
- The further development may be squeezed into the last never ending maintenance phase (as enhancement requests). This may virtually run without a proper process.

Agile Development

Agile Project Management is a method of delivering projects in a highly flexible and interactive manner. It is derived from Agile Software Development standards. It is a variant of iterative life cycle where deliverables are submitted in stages in weeks as shown in Figure 1.3. There are several variants in Agile, including Scrum and Extreme Programming.

Given as follows are four distinct items of Agile Manifesto which need to be addressed by the methodology:

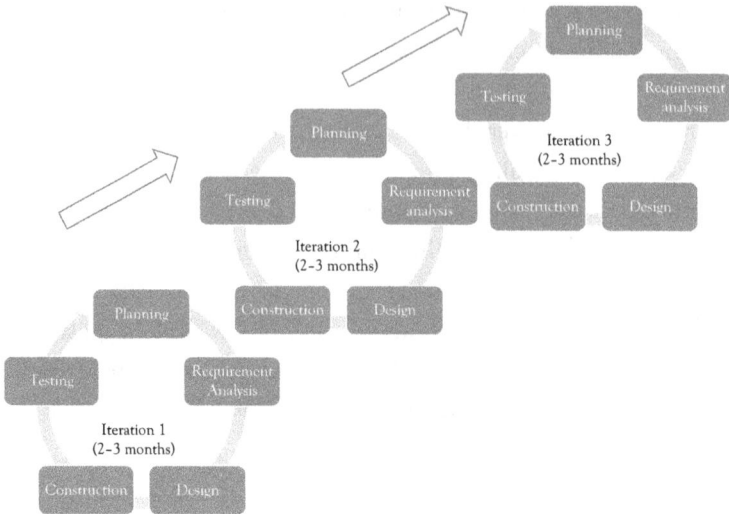

Figure 1.3 Agile development with iterations

Individuals and Interactions: In Agile development, self-organization and motivation are important. Interactions among team members are increased with colocation and pair programming.

Working software: In Agile, delivering a piece of working software to clients is more important than presenting a piece of document in the meeting.

Customer collaboration: In Agile, continuous customer or stakeholder involvement is very important (as all the requirements cannot be collected at the beginning of the software development cycle).

Responding to change: There has to be quick responses to change and continuous development in Agile development environment.

Advantages and Disadvantages of Agile

Waterfall, as a Project Management methodology, has been criticized for not being able to cope with constant changes in software projects. The iterative nature of Agile makes it an excellent alternative when it comes to managing software projects. Agile, however, has its disadvantages. As many believe that it doesn't scale well, waterfall methodology is still used for many large software projects.

Role of a Project Manager

Project management is the discipline where the knowledge, skills, tools, and techniques are applied to project activities to take the project from concept to completion. In general, project managers have the responsibility to lead and manage the team to achieve the project objectives. In doing so, they also have to satisfy the needs of various stakeholders like customers, sponsors, and team members in a balanced manner. As project management is a critical strategic discipline, the project manager's role involves achieving the strategic objectives using the team.

What knowledge and skills are required for the project manager or project management team? To manage projects effectively, there are five areas of expertise needed.

These five areas are:

1. Knowledge of project management processes, and tools like MS-Project.
2. Knowledge of application area like Information Technology, Automotive Product Development.
3. Understanding of project environment like political environment.
4. General management skills like marketing.
5. Interpersonal skills like motivating the team.

These areas are not distinct and may generally overlap.

Project Management and MS-Project

As we discussed in the earlier section, skills related to tools like MS-Project are part of the essential skills of a project manager. The project manager also has the responsibility of engaging stakeholders and managing their expectations. MS-Project can help a project manager in doing that.

Project information				
Professional planner / cost accountant	Project manager	Owner/ client	Executive	Contractor

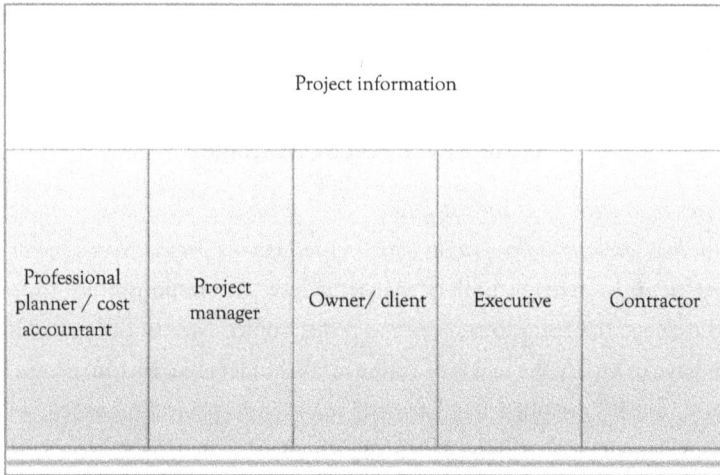

Figure 1.4 MS Project helps to share project information with various project stakeholders

Many engineers tend to believe that a tool like MS-Project is used only for scheduling. However, it has utility much beyond scheduling. It is very important that projects are managed in an integrated way. For this to happen, the critical and relevant project information should be shared across all departments and also with various stakeholders. Software like MS-Project helps in achieving the same as depicted in Figure 1.4. Because of this, various stakeholders like team members, project managers, and suppliers can be on the same page. Finally, this reduces risks and increases profitability.

How do tools like MS-Project help various stakeholders? Management needs a macro level view of the project through reports like Milestone reports (delivered via e-mail or interactive browsers). Although very senior professionals like general managers and vice presidents do not schedule the project themselves, they may want customizable project information. MS-Project displays project schedule and cost metrics so that project profitability can be improved. Various financial reports (like cash flow over time) can be generated during planning; helping project sponsors forecast the cash flow.

Project schedulers and planners can use MS-Project to schedule projects with ease, to establish company standards using company-specific templates, and to perform baseline analysis to understand exact project costs. As MS-Project supports consolidating multiple projects, schedulers can easily consolidate subcontractor schedules. MS-Project provides project schedulers with the basic tools to easily plan and control projects.

Planning and controlling a small project may be easy. However, planning and controlling a large project are not easy. Schedulers can quickly create optimum project plans and zero in to understand the critical path in large network diagrams. They can easily create "what-if?" project scenarios to simulate possible adjustments, including compressing the schedule with fast tracking (to work in parallel). MS-Project enables schedulers to examine an activity—and its predecessors and successors. It helps to determine why an activity is scheduled at a particular time, and answer questions such as: Were any of its predecessors delayed? Do any of its predecessors or successors have constraints?

MS-Project also helps a project team in various processes related to other knowledge areas (other than project schedule or time management) as well. Figure 1.5 shows how MS-Project helps in managing various processes related to different knowledge areas of the project. It helps the project team to identify, quantify, and mitigate risks such as late supply of hardware, or additional software installations. Risks can be categorized and control plans can be documented as part of the overall project plan. MS-Project also helps teams prepare for the unexpected

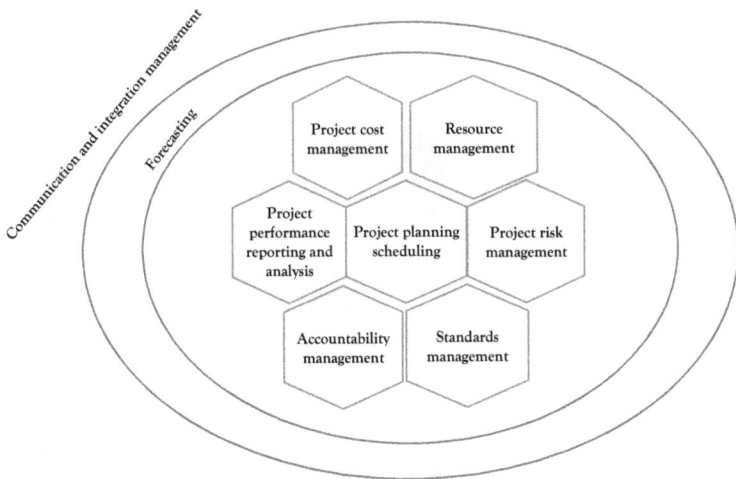

Figure 1.5 MS-Project helps in various Project Management processes of different knowledge areas

through a "what-if?" project and resource-simulation engine to determine the schedule and cost exposure of project risks. With this information, project managers and schedulers can flag potential risks and take necessary steps to plan an appropriate response.

Many of these features, right from creating and using templates to managing multiple projects, have been discussed in this book, with guided examples. We will be looking at this in detail in subsequent chapters.

To conclude, we looked at a project life cycle, different software process models and skill sets required for a project manager in this chapter. We also understood (at a macrolevel) how MS-Project can help various stakeholders.

CHAPTER 2

Scope Management

Objectives

On completion of this chapter, you should be able to

1. Understand what is meant by project scope management
2. Understand the difference between project scope and product scope
3. Know various scope management processes
4. Understand what is meant by work breakdown structure(WBS) and WBS dictionary
5. Learn how to use MS-Project to create WBS

Scope is one of the key objectives of the project along with schedule, cost, quality, and so on. It is important to define the scope of the project, to plan the schedule and the cost of the project. That is why some key planning processes are related to scope management.

What Is Scope Management?

The goal of the project scope management is to ensure that all the required work and only the required work are included and executed in the project. Hence, scope management consists of processes to ensure that the requirements of the customer and other stakeholders are captured in a specification of work.

Project Scope Versus Product Scope

The scope of a project consists of the project scope and the product scope as shown in Figure 2.1. The project scope is defined as the work that must be performed to deliver the required products, services, or results with the

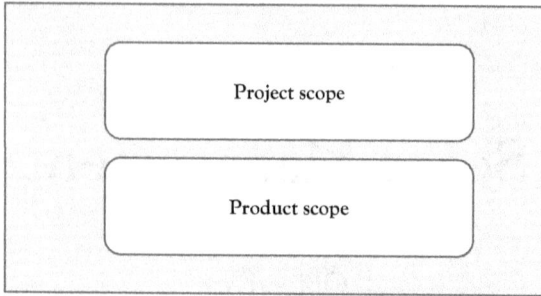

Figure 2.1 Project scope is not the same thing as the product scope. Project scope is the work required to deliver the product scope

specified functions and features. The product scope is the set of functions and features that characterize a product, service, or result to be delivered by the current project.

For example, if you are purchasing and deploying a software in a bank to streamline various day-to-day operations, specifications like the software should be able to manage various operations related to savings bank accounts, fixed deposit accounts of a million customers, and so on, form the part of the product scope. Tasks like hiring a consultant, preparing a bid document, and so on, form the part of the project scope.

Project Scope Management Processes

These six processes mentioned subsequently are part of the project scope management according to the *Project Management Body of Knowledge* (*PMBOK*):

1. *Plan scope management*—Document how the project scope is defined, validated, and controlled.
2. *Collect requirements*—Define the project and product requirements and develop a plan to manage those requirements. Project stakeholders' list is an input for collecting requirements. This will help clarify what needs to be done.
3. *Define scope*—Develop a detailed description of the project and the product that will determine what needs to be done by the project team.

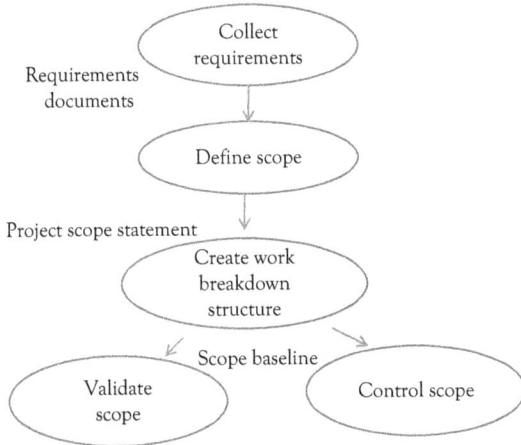

Figure 2.2 Relation among project scope management processes

4. *Create work breakdown structure (WBS)*—Break down the scope into concrete, easily manageable components. This logically completes the scope base lining.

5. *Validate scope*—Formalize the acceptance of the completed project deliverables. Identify how you will verify that the project scope has been executed as planned.

6. *Control scope*—Determine how to monitor the status of the project and product scope and monitor and control changes to the scope.

Let us look at the illustration shown in Figure 2.2 to understand how some of these processes are related and what key outputs these processes produce.

We will study the key process of creating WBS and using MS-Project to create WBS in subsequent sections.

Create WBS

As you know, information technology projects may cost millions of dollars and take hundreds of person years of effort. It is not easy to schedule, estimate, and track such projects. How do you ensure that all the work defined as the scope of the project is accounted for? The answer lies in creating and using a WBS. It ensures that the work is decomposed into

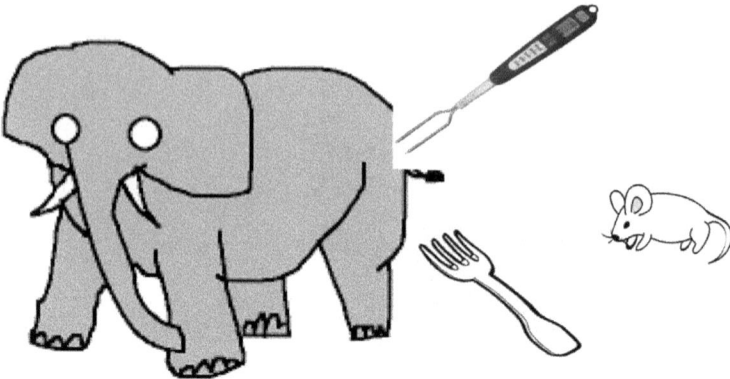

Figure 2.3 Creating a WBS is like eating an elephant byte by byte

small enough packages. To give an analogy, creating a WBS is like eating an elephant one byte at a time (Figure 2.3).

In a project, a WBS is represented as an elaborate outline, providing each task with a WBS code that identifies where it falls within your project plan. The product-specific work and process-specific work are broken into small manageable components, as illustrated in Figure 2.4. Note that the sequence of the work does not matter at this stage. Creating a quality WBS may take substantial amount of time and generally involves brainstorming of stakeholders.

A WBS for a large project will have multiple levels of detail, and the lowest WBS element will be linked to functional area cost accounts that are made up of individual work packages. Whether you need three levels

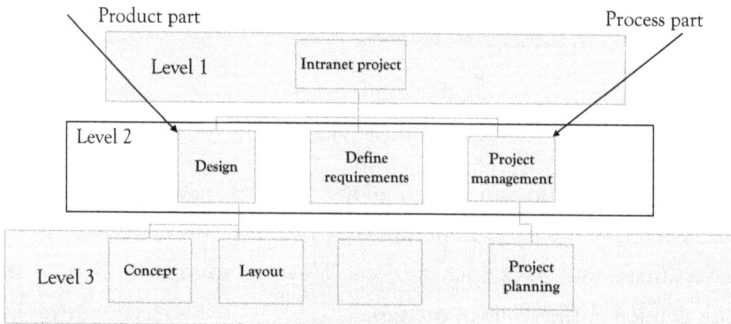

Figure 2.4 WBS: product and process parts

or eight, work packages should add up through each WBS level to form the project total.

WBS Numbering and WBS Dictionary

WBS elements are usually numbered, and the numbering system may be arranged the way you choose. In a WBS code, each indent level in your task structure is given a set of letters, numbers, or characters that you define. For example, the phases may be given a set of characters; the tasks may be given a number; and the subtasks may be given a lowercase letter.

In a project, you can also assign a prefix for the code, to indicate the task's project. The sample WBS of a retail website project (Figure 2.5) illustrates the use of prefixes in identifying components of a WBS. Hence, the box numbered 123.1.1 will tell you that it is in the first box in level 1,and is the first box in level 2 of the project numbered 123.

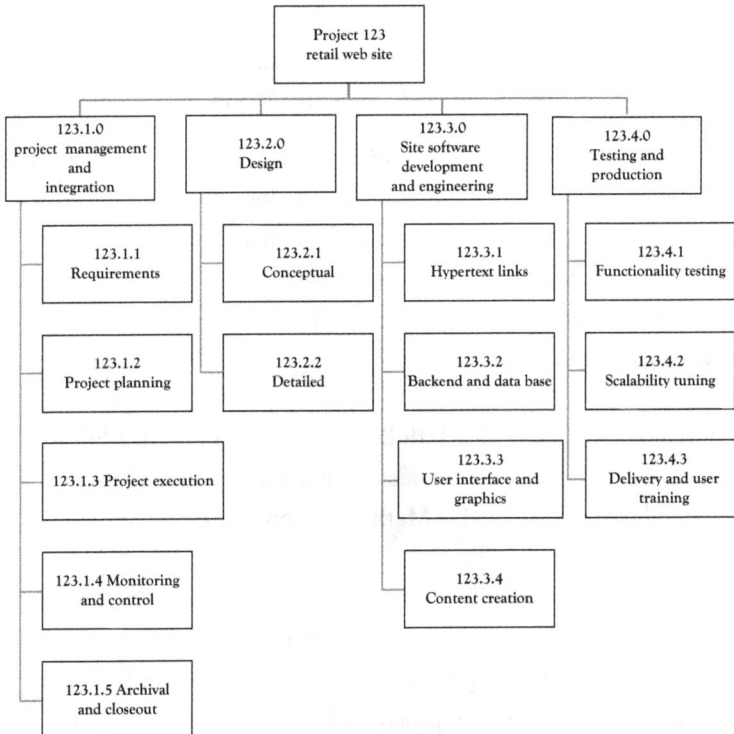

Figure 2.5 Sample WBS of a retail website project

If a WBS is extensive and if the category content is not obvious to the project team members, it may be useful to write a WBS dictionary. The WBS dictionary describes what is in each WBS element, and it may also say what is not in an element, if that is unclear. Here is a sample of a WBS dictionary description:

> *WBS Element 123.1.1.—Requirements—This element includes the effort to gather various requirements related to the website. These requirements include various stakeholder requirements (like user, administrator, and server-owner). It does not include the work required to write design specifications of the website.*

In MS-Project, one can use subtasks and summary tasks to decompose project-related work. MS-Project also provides features to assign WBS codes. Let us do an exercise to find out how MS-Project can be used to assign WBS codes in a Project.

Example Problem: Generating WBS Codes for a Task List in a Project

In the example problem, we are going to use a project called Math lib which has partially built task lists (with a specific hierarchy). This already has some summary tasks and subtasks for a mathematical library development. The purpose of this is to demonstrate how we can build a WBS code structure (and display the same) and WBS numbers in MS-Project professional.

- Copy the project file **Math lib original** from **Practice-Files/ Ch02** to your working directory. Rename the file as **Math lib**. Double click on the file **Math lib**, to open it in MS-Project 2016.
- As a first step we will generate codes for the tasks using a simple coding system known as outline number. Outline numbers offer a simple and primitive coding system for the project. These are auto generated in MS-Project based on the task level (indentation) and you cannot change these directly.

You cannot use characters and alphabets for outline numbers, as it is too primitive a system. Outline numbers have to be numeric. To display outline numbers, on the **Format** tab, in the **Show/Hide** group, select the check-box **Outline Number**. Outline numbers get displayed adjacent to each task, in the task name column itself as shown in Figure 2.6.

- Next we will create a custom WBS code, which can also have alphabets and special characters. For this we have to create a code mask and only this single code mask will be used for the entire project.

- On the **Project** tab, in the **Properties** group, click on the **WBS** button. Select **Define Code** from the drop-down, as shown in Figure 2.7.

You will get the WBS Code Definition dialog box, as shown in the illustration (Figure 2.8). This dialog box has to be used to define and format a WBS code structure. This will also help to preview the code

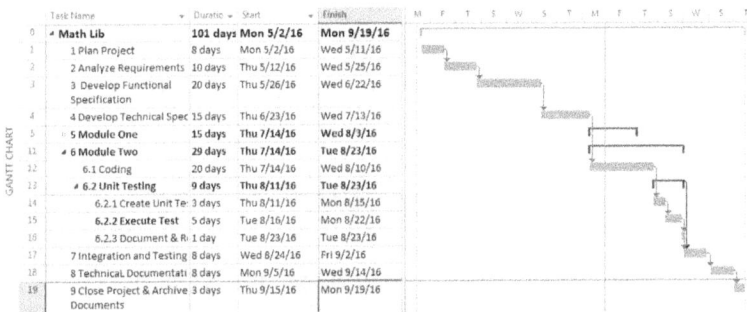

Figure 2.6 Display outline numbers using the check-box from the Show/Hide group under the Format tab

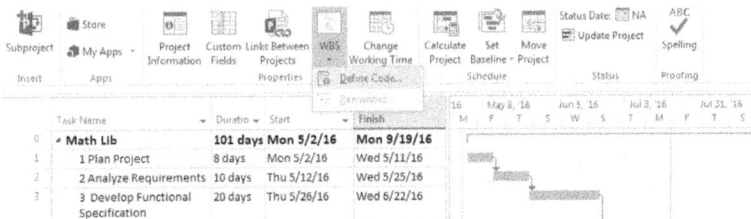

Figure 2.7 Menu for initiating WBS definition

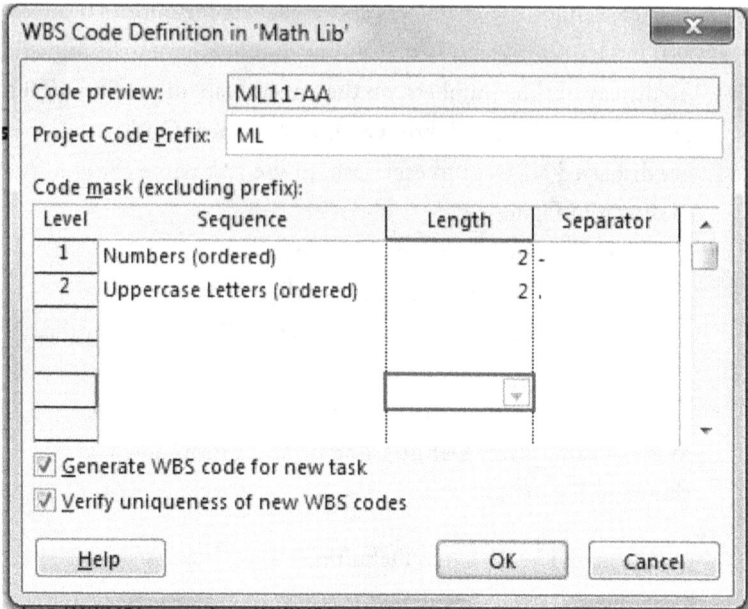

WBS Code Definition in 'Math Lib'   ✕

Code preview: ML11-AA

Project Code Prefix: ML

Code mask (excluding prefix):

Level	Sequence	Length	Separator	▲
1	Numbers (ordered)	2	-	
2	Uppercase Letters (ordered)	2	.	
		▼		
				▼

☑ Generate WBS code for new task
☑ Verify uniqueness of new WBS codes

| Help | | OK | Cancel |

Figure 2.8 Use code-mask table to define WBS in the dialog box

generated. In this example, we use the code ML (representing Math Lib) for the project. However, one may use any other code based on clients' specifications, company standards, and so on.

- Type Project Code *ML* in the appropriate text box. We can preview the WBS code of a task at the lowermost level as an example, in the code preview box as we build out our WBS code structure. We can use the columns and rows in the Code mask table to build out our WBS code structure. Each row represents an indent level for tasks in your project. You have to specify sequence, length, and separator at each level using the drop-down menus (refer the box for more information and options).

- Here we want to generate a code like ML11-AA, the Project Code being ML. As you observe, the level 1 is numeric and is having a length of 2 (in this code example 11). The level 2 is also of length 2 and consists of uppercase characters (in this code example *AA*). They are separated by a separator "-".

Sequence

- Numbers (ordered)—Sequential numbers will be inserted by MS-Project, for this part of the code. You can edit these numbers later.

- Uppercase Letters (ordered)—Sequential uppercase letters will be inserted by MS-Project.

- Lowercase Letters (ordered)—Sequential lowercase letters will be inserted by MS-Project.

- Characters (unordered)—MS-Project will insert an asterisk (*). You can go back and change it to any character later.

Length

- If you want to edit this part of the code later using a variety of number of characters, select *Any*.

- If you want to set a fixed number of characters for this section of formatting, select *1* through *10* (e.g., if you select *1*, you will specify up to nine subtasks at this level. If you specify two you will be able to specify up to 99 subtasks at this level).

Separator

- Identify a separator from the choices in the drop-down menu or type another symbol directly on the keyboard.

Select Numbers (ordered) for level 1 and Uppercase letters (ordered) for level 2. There are not too many phases and subtasks. Specify 2 as length for both rows. Use "-" and "." as separators. Select the Generate WBS code for new task check-box if you want to create a WBS code automatically for each task you add to your project.

- If you want each WBS code to be unique, select the **Verify uniqueness of new WBS codes** check-box. If you have used the Characters option in the Sequence column, this can help to avoid duplication of codes. Click **OK** and this shall generate the WBS code structure.

- Now the code structure has been defined. However, WBS code is yet to be displayed in the Gantt Chart view. Though you can insert a column anywhere in the table, we shall display the WBS code just adjacent to the Task Mode in this

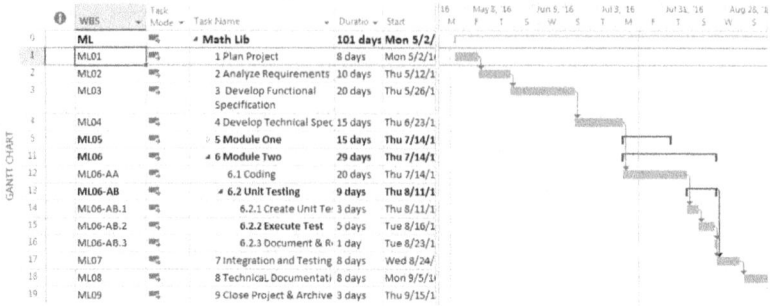

Figure 2.9 WBS column displays the WBS code for each task

case. This is done by right clicking on the column header of the Task Mode column and selecting **Insert column** from the dynamic menu. Select **WBS**. You will be getting WBS column with appropriate codes in the Gantt Chart as shown in Figure 2.9.

• Close the **Math Lib** file.

Some More WBS Resources

Project Management Institute: Practice Standard for Work Breakdown Structures is available on the website of PMI (www.pmi.org).

Military Standard for WBS: For comprehensive instructions on how to build a WBS, check out the complete military standard for WBS on the Every Spec website www.everyspec.comand just search for WBS.

If your project has already been entered in MS-Project, you may want to consider a third-party add-on for MS-Project to convert a Gantt Chart task list with indents into a standard WBS graphic. There are some packages available in the market for the same.

To conclude, we discussed about the use of WBS in scope management and also with the guided example and studied how we could generate custom WBS codes for all tasks in the entire project.

CHAPTER 3

Introduction to Project Scheduling

Objectives

On completion of this chapter, you should be able to

1. Understand what is meant by activity sequencing
2. Understand how network diagrams are used in scheduling
3. Understand different types of relationships between tasks (activities)
4. Learn how to use Project templates to jump start planning in MS-Project

In Chapter 2, we studied about creating a work breakdown structure (WBS). The WBS will help you to baseline the scope of the project. However, you have yet to arrive with the schedule of the project. There are five key project planning processes (according to *Project Management Body of Knowledge* [*PMBOK*]) that will help you to arrive at the schedule once you are ready with the scope of the work. These are:

- Define activities
- Sequence activities
- Estimate activity resources
- Estimate activity durations
- Develop a schedule

In this chapter, we will discuss about how to define activities and how to arrive at a sequence of activities. In subsequent chapters, we shall discuss about estimating activity resources and durations, and also arriving at a schedule. (Note that some of these processes may be combined together in some organizations, based on the organization's own practices and parameters such as the project size and the domain.)

Define Activities

The first process in the activity planning section is *define activities*. This process starts with the WBS and identifies the activities required to produce the various project deliverables. Activities are viewed from the perspective of the work packages. You ask the question, "What activities are required to come out with deliverables of the work package?" In the next process, the resulting information from this process is used to organize the activities into a specific sequence. Let us take the example of website requirements work package. This particular work package can be decomposed into activities like user requirements and content requirements as shown in Figure 3.1. As an outcome of this process, you will get activity list and attributes. In MS-Project, as we discussed, all activities are represented by tasks. However, you can use *summary tasks* to represent work packages and subtasks to represent activities. (For more information on how to insert a summary task using MS-Project, you may refer Appendix C, *A quick introduction to MS-Project 2016*). You will also get a milestones list in the project. In a project, milestones are significant

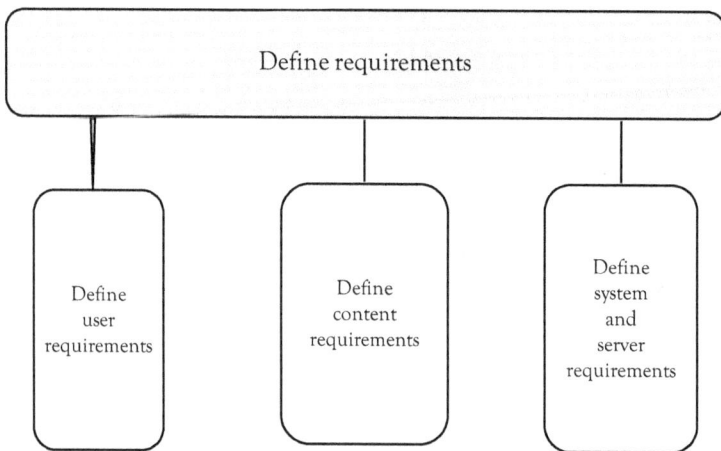

Figure 3.1 An example of breaking up website requirements work package into activities

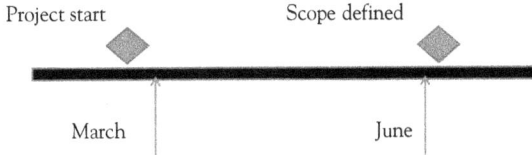

Figure 3.2 Milestones along the timeline of a project

events or points of interest (Figure 3.2).Milestones have zero duration. For example, project start and design freeze are milestones in a project.

Project milestones are also referred to as a Phase Gate, Stage Gate, Check Point, or Decision Point. In MS-Project, in Gantt Chart, milestones are represented using a diamond shape, by default.

Sequence Activities

The next process is that of arranging the activity list from activity definition into a discrete sequence (Figure 3.3). Some activities can be accomplished at any time throughout the project. Other activities depend on input from another activity or are constrained by time or resources. Any requirement that restricts the start or end time of an activity is a logical relationship. This process identifies all relationships between activities and notes restrictions imposed by these relationships.

For example, when building a software you cannot do unit testing of a module unless the coding is completed for the same. This is just one

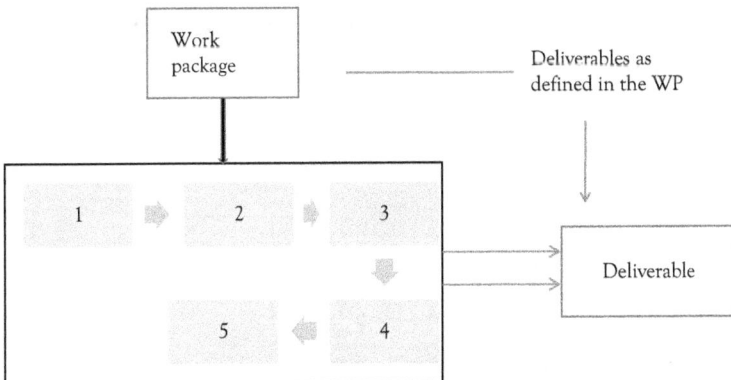

Figure 3.3 Sequencing of activities in a work-package

example of how activities can be related to one another. The sequence activities process is one that can benefit from the use of computer software to assist in noting and keeping track of interactivity relationships.

Network Diagrams and Precedence Diagramming Method

When planning project activities, as a first step, we have to understand network diagrams. *Network diagrams* provide a graphical view of activities and how they are related to one another. The most common type of diagramming method for building a schedule network diagram is the precedence diagramming method (PDM). Activity on node (AON) is a PDM. Most scheduling software packages use AON. A sample AON is shown in Figure 3.4 for reference.

The PDM shows nodes—representing activities—connected by arrows that represent logical relationships. For example, to represent that activity B is dependent on activity A (in other words, activity A must be complete before activity B starts), simply draw an arrow from A to B. PDM diagrams are also referred to as AON diagrams because the nodes contain the activity duration information. The arrows show how some activities are dependent on other activities. For example, activity D cannot start until activities C and E are complete. To show this dual dependency, we draw an arrow from C to D and another arrow from E to D.

In fact, nodes generally contain several pieces of information, including

- **Early start**—The earliest date the activity can start
- **Duration**—The duration of the activity

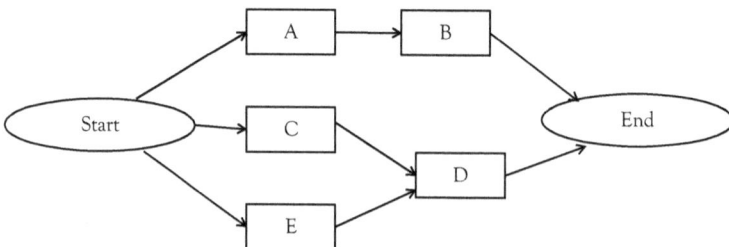

Figure 3.4 An example of an AON diagram

- **Early finish**—The earliest date the activity can finish
- **Late start**—The latest date the activity can start
- **Late finish**—The latest date the activity can finish
- **Float or slack**—Difference between the early start and the late start dates (or the difference between early finish and late finish dates)

We will discuss about the same and also will see how this can be used in schedule-related computations in subsequent chapters.

There can be four types of relationships with a PDM diagram, as shown in Figure 3.5:

- **Finish-to-start**—It is the most common type of dependency. The successor activity's start depends on the completion of the predecessor activity. For example, finish coding for Module 1 before starting unit testing Module 1.

▸ Start-to-finish

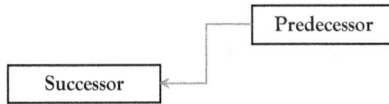

▸ Start-to-start

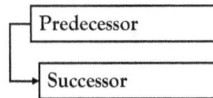

▸ Finish to start

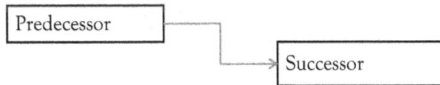

▸ Finish to finish

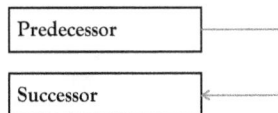

Figure 3.5 Different types of relationships between tasks (activities)

- **Finish-to-finish**—The completion of the successor activity depends on the completion of the predecessor activity. Let us say you are doing a series of tests and creating a test report. The test report cannot be finished unless testing activity is finished.
- **Start-to-start**—The start of the successor activity depends on the start of the predecessor activity. You have to start integration of modules to start integration testing.
- **Start-to-finish**—The completion of the successor activity depends on the start of the predecessor activity. It is rarely used.

Leads and Lags

In addition to relationships, we have to understand the two terms related to time period, namely lead and lag to build a schedule network (see Figure 3.6). A successor activity can be advanced with respect to a predecessor activity, when you have a lead. For example, if you are writing a big proposal, two weeks before finishing the first draft, the review process can be started. This would be shown as a finish-to-start relationship with a two weeks' lead.

When you have a lag, a successor activity will be delayed with respect to a predecessor activity. For example, let us say you are building two modules of software using a new tool. Though these can be started

Example of a lead

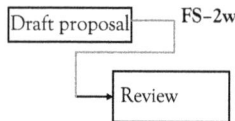

Example of a lag

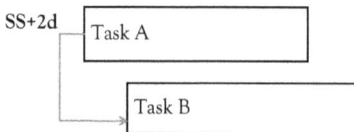

Figure 3.6 Example of lead and lag

simultaneously, you are delaying the Task B of building Module 2 because you want to apply the learning of building Module 1 (of Task A), as shown in Figure 3.6. The use of leads and lag is purely based on technical requirements and constraints. It should not replace schedule logic.

Project Templates

We discussed about activity lists and sequencing in this chapter. Although no two projects can be the same, there can be similar projects. For example, different Mobile AppDevelopment projects can have same tasks and sequences. It means that you may use a *template* that includes much of the initial information you need, like task (activity) names and relationships, to jump-start project planning. This can help you to expedite the process of arriving at the activity list and sequencing the same. We will be discussing the same with an example in the next section.

Sources of templates can vary. Some templates installed during the installation of MS-Project templates are also available on MS-Office online website, *www.office.com*, and other industry-specific websites. To see such available templates online, click on **File** tab and then **New.** You also see a search box to facilitate the search. (You may require a change in security settings of MS-Project, for the same. Click on **File** Tab and select **Options**. Click on the **Trust Center** in **Project Options Dialog** that pops up, and click on the button **Trust Center Settings**. Ensure that the **Allow office to connect to the Internet** is selected under **Privacy Options** of the Trust Center.)

Templates may also be shared with you by other MS-Project users you know (who may be doing similar projects). Organizations also provide templates to the employees based on the typical projects they execute.

Example Problem: Using Templates to Expedite the Planning

You can also create templates from your project plans for later use or to share with say your vendors or your organization. We will be discussing about the same in this example and also see how you can avoid passing sensitive information in the template file.

1. Copy Sample Project file **Porting-original.mpp** from the **Practice-Files/Ch03** folder and rename as **Porting.mpp**. Double click and open the file. Take a look at the task list in the Gantt Chart view (Figure 3.7). View the resource information in the Resource sheet view. You will see information like resource name and resource rate (Figure 3.8).

2. On the **File** tab, click **Save As**. Navigate to the folder in which you want to save the new template. In the **Save as Type** box, select **Project Template**. In the **File Name** box, enter the template file name that you want, and then click **Save** (Figure 3.9).

3. Information like Resource pay rates may be sensitive and you may be having concerns on sharing the same with say other departments, your suppliers, or business associates. When the **Save As Template** dialog box appears, select the type of information, such as resource rates (Figure 3.10), which you want to be removed from the template. Note that the original project plan is not affected. After selecting the data like resource rates using the check-box, click on **Save.** The template gets saved with an extension .*mpt*.

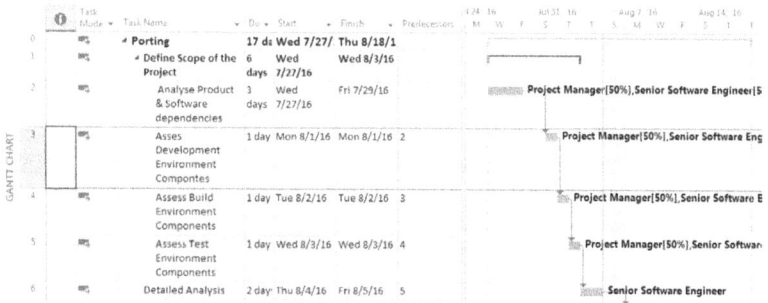

Figure 3.7 Task list in the Gantt Chart view of the original file (typical project)

Figure 3.8 Resource sheet view of the original file (typical project)

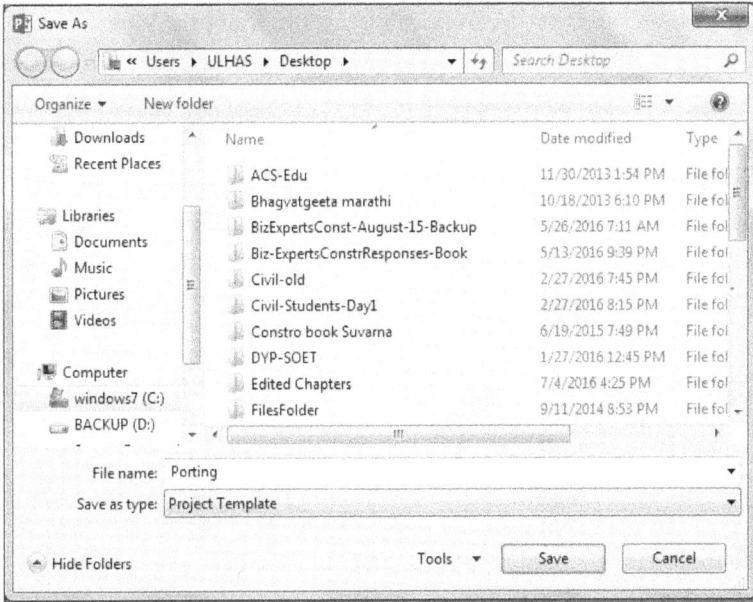

Figure 3.9 Save the file as a project template

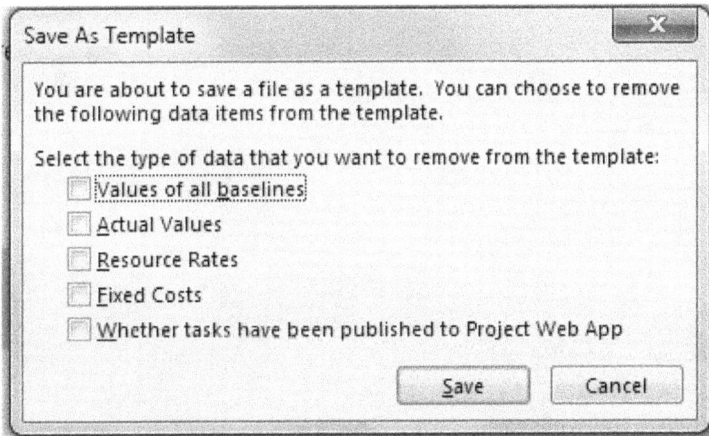

Figure 3.10 Save as template dialog enables you to remove data from the template when you are saving

4. As a last step, you may verify the Resource sheet of the template file you created. View the Gantt Chart. You will find all the tasks listed. When you view the Resource sheet of the template file (Click **View**

Tab and then on **Resource Sheet** in **the Resource Views** Group), you will find that information like resource rates are listed as null as seen in Figure 3.11. Close both files.

To conclude, we discussed about various processes related to scheduling and also looked at sequencing in detail, in this chapter. As an example, we saw how MS-Project templates can be used to jump-start the project planning with activity lists and sequencing.

	Resource Name	Type	Material	Initials	Group	Max.	Std. Rate	Ovt.	Cost/Use	Accrue	Base
1	Project Manager	Work		P		100%	$0.00/hr	$0.00/hr	$0.00	Prorated	Standard
2	Senior Software Engineer	Work		S		100%	$0.00/hr	$0.00/hr	$0.00	Prorated	Standard
3	Software Engineer	Work		S		100%	$0.00/hr	$0.00/hr	$0.00	Prorated	Standard
4	Test Engineer	Work		T		100%	$0.00/hr	$0.00/hr	$0.00	Prorated	Standard

Figure 3.11 Information like resource rate has been removed and is not available in the template

CHAPTER 4

Resources

Objectives

On completion of this chapter, you should be able to

1. Understand various types of resources that exist in MS-Project
2. Understand how to create and assign resources in a project using MS-Project

Once the sequence of tasks (activities) is known, the next step is to prepare the Resource Sheet indicating resources which may possibly be assigned to various tasks. This may not be a necessary step, only when you do not have any resources in house and outsource the entire work. This is not the case with most of the projects and a key constraint of many projects is resources. Assigning resources and estimating durations have to be done in all such cases to develop the project schedule.

Understanding the Resource Sheet

Here is an explanation of various fields of Resource sheet[1] (see Box)

Assigning Resources

Once the resources are created in the Resource Sheet, the project planner or project manager assigns these resources. Assigning resources can be done in more than one way and we will be learning one of the ways of assigning resources (using split view) here in this chapter. We will also be discussing about different task types later, in this chapter, using the same project file.

Terms

Resources: People, Equipment, and Consumable items (like printer cartridges, Compact Disks, Paper) used to complete the project tasks.

Resource Name: Assign the name of the resource. You will see this name beside the Gantt Chart bar. At times, these can be based on the role or function also (like programmer and project manager).

Resource Types:

Work:

(i) Human resource, like employees, consultants, analysts, engineers

(ii) Equipment which are charged on hourly or daily basis, like computers

Material: The supplies or other consumable items that are used to complete tasks like paper, compact disks.

Cost: It is the single expense of the project. (Counted by the usage like traveling expenses, licensing fees).

Material Label: Identify the quantity of the material that will be consumed. This field is only workable if resource type is material. Unit of measure is mentioned here. For example, Rims in case of Paper, Numbers in case of Compact Disks.

Initials: Project will automatically generate it as a single character (can be and should be set appropriately).

Group: Identify whether the resource belongs to a particular department for example, Testing. This will help to display or filter resources better.

Max. Units: A percentage that indicates the resource s allocation in daily scheduled work (by default, it is 100 percent meaning Single Person working Full time; 40 hours/week).

Std. Rate: The amount shows how much cost is added to the project for each hour of work using a resource.

Ovt. Rate: Overtime (OT) cost for a work resource.

Cost/ Use: Set the charge of a material resource per use.

Base Calendar: Set the type of the calendar, standard (by default), 24 hours or night shift.

> *Code*: Identify the resources.
>
> Specifies how the Project accounts for the timing of resource costs in the budget.
>
> *Accrue At:*
>
> Prorated (By default): Project adds in costs at the time when work is scheduled.
>
> Start: Cost is paid before the work starts.
>
> End: Cost is paid after the work ends.

Example Problem: Assigning Resources Using Split View

In this exercise, we will be assigning a resource to a task using split view. The purpose is to understand the process of assigning a work resource to a task. A simple project file containing a single task (Test Execution) has been created for the purpose. The file has a work resource called Testing Engineer.

1. Copy the file **ResourceAlloc1-orginal.mpp** from **Practice-files/ Ch04** directory to your working directory and rename it as **ResourceAlloc1.mpp**. Double click on the file. You will see the Gantt Chart containing an auto-scheduled task called Test Execution (Figure 4.1).

2. Switch to Resource Sheet view by using **View Buttons** on the right hand side bottom corner (near zoom slider). You will observe that there is a single resource called Testing Engineer (Figure 4.2). The task *Test Execution* has to be assigned with the resource Testing Engineer.

3. Switch back to **Gantt Chart** by using View Buttons on the right-hand side bottom corner (near zoom slider). Let us take a closer look

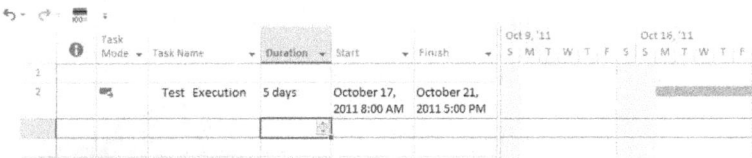

Figure 4.1 Gantt Chart of the project with a single auto-scheduled task Test Execution

🛈	Resource Name ▾	Type ▾	Materi Label ▾	Initials ▾	Grou ▾	Max. Units ▾	Std. Rate ▾	Ovt. Rate ▾	Cost/Use ▾	Accrue At ▾	Base Calendar ▾	Code ▾
2	Testing Engineer	Work		T		100%	$1.00/hr	$1.00/hr	$0.00	Prorated	Standard	

Figure 4.2 Resource Sheet view of the project

of the *Test Execution* task. For this, a view called Task form will be handy.

4. On the **View** tab, in the **Split View** group, select the **Details** check-box (Figure 4.3). Project splits the window into two panes. In the upper pane is the Gantt Chart view, and below it is the Task Form view. You will get the details of the selected task, *Test Execution* Click anywhere in the **Task Form** view and then, on the **Format** tab, in the **Details** group, click **Work**. The Work details appear.

Task Form is a handy way to see a task's duration, units, and work values. As of now, there is no Resource assigned in the Task Form view. As you assign resources, you can see the essential scheduling values for the task *Test Execution.*

5. Click in the **Resource Name** column of the **Task Form** and you will see an arrow on the right edge of the row. When you click on the arrow (pull down), the list of resources appears. In this case, the only resource available is *Testing Engineer.* Select the same (Figure 4.4).

6. In MS-Project, you have the option of computing the work when you assign the resources or unassign the resources. By default, tasks in MS-Project are not effort driven. Select the **Effort driven** by using the check-box on the top of the task form. It means, as more resources are assigned to the task, the duration decreases, but the total work remains the same and is distributed among the assigned resources (see the following box for more information on effort-driven scheduling).

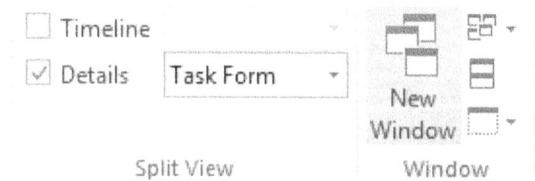

☐ Timeline		
☑ Details	Task Form ▾	
	Split View	New Window	Window

Figure 4.3 Use the details check-box to view the Task Form

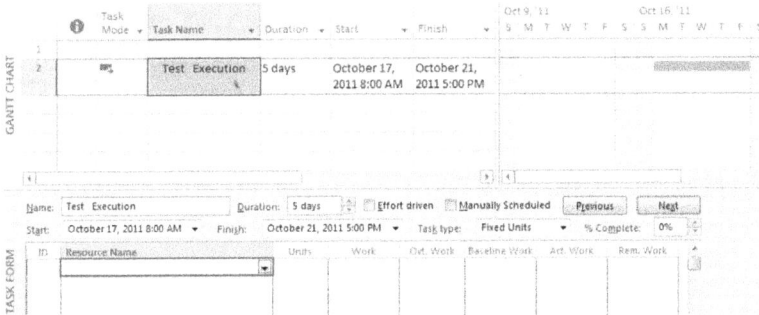

Figure 4.4 Task form also helps to assign resources

7. You will see on the Gantt Chart that *Testing Engineer* is associated with the Test—Execution task (Figure 4.5). The name of the resource appears next to the task bar too. You can deselect the **Details** checkbox in the **Split views** group (in the **View** tab) and close the task form.

8. Save the file. However, you need not close the session and the project file, as we will be doing some more exercises.

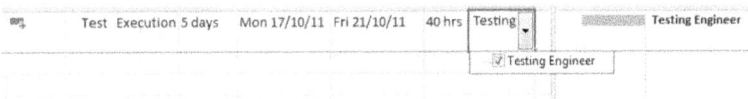

Figure 4.5 Assigned resources are seen next to the task bar

Effort-Driven Tasks and the Scheduling Formula

By default, effort-driven scheduling is disabled for all tasks you create in MS-Project. This implies that when you add or remove resources, the duration of the task does not get affected and the quantum of work done is not changed. For example, let us say five people attend a meeting of one hour as a part of the project. By adding five more people for the task *Meeting*, you will not be able to reduce the time to half an hour. Ten people attending the meeting may not mean that more project-related work is done.

You can turn on effort-driven scheduling for an entire project plan or just for a few select tasks. In subsequent sections, we will study how we can use Actions list to control recalculation of the work on a task imme-diately after assigning or unassigning resources. Effort-driven scheduling is applicable only when you assign additional resources to or remove resources from *Automatically scheduled* tasks.

MS-Project uses the following **scheduling formula** to compute the work:

Duration × Assignment units = Work

Let us look at the specific example and find these values in the Task Form. The duration of task *Test Execution* is five working days, which equals 40 hours. When you assigned a Testing Engineer to task *Test Execution*, MS-Project applied 100 percent of Test Engineer's working time to this task. The scheduling formula for the *Test Execution* task looks like this:

40 hour (the same as 5 days) task duration × 100 percent assignment units = 40 hour of work

Types of Tasks

Tasks can also be classified in a different way into three categories, namely, Fixed Units, Fixed Duration, and Fixed Work.

A *Fixed Units* task (Figure 4.6) is a task in which the assigned units (or resources) are a fixed value, and any changes to the amount of work or the task's duration do not affect the task's units.

Let us continue with our example and experiment a bit to understand this better. By default, the effort-driven tasks created are of type *Fixed Units*. The *Test Execution* task is also of type *Fixed Units*.

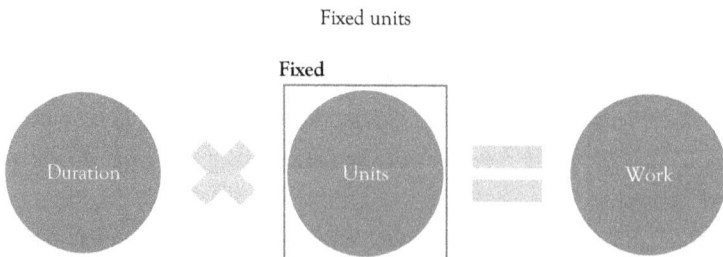

Figure 4.6 Conceptual view of fixed units task

1. Click on the Durations field of *Test Execution* job and make Duration 10 days. You will get an **Actions** button (on the left) with the Actions list as shown in Figure 4.7. (Actions list will give you an option to change the response of MS-Project.)
2. The default option is to keep units the same and increase the work. Select the same. With this, you have one Test Engineer working for 10 days. This option appeared as a default, because the task type was *Fixed Units*. Select the same with the help of the cursor and the Action button disappears. You may save and close the project file.

Fixed Duration task is a task in which the duration is a fixed value and any changes to the work or the assigned units (i.e., resources) do not affect the task's duration (Figure 4.8).

A *Fixed Work* task is a task in which the amount of work is a fixed value and any changes to the task's duration or the number of assigned units (or resources) do not affect the task's work (Figure 4.9).

To conclude, we did discuss about assigning resources and also about task types in Microsoft Project in this chapter.

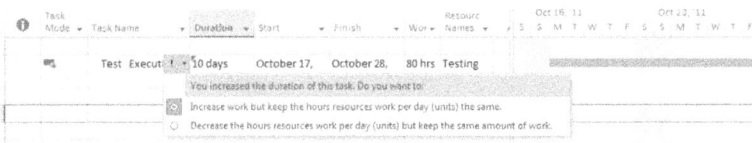

Figure 4.7 Action buttons help you to control the outcome when you change the duration, units, and so on

Note: You may explore other two task types, on similar lines. For brevity, we are limiting the discussion over here.

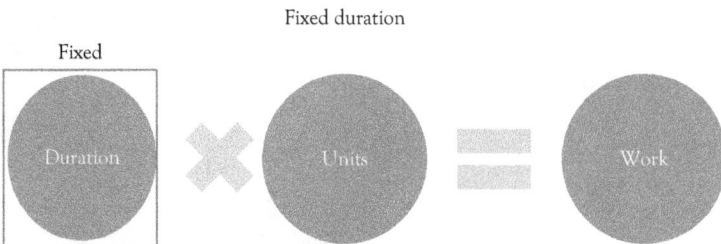

Figure 4.8 Conceptual view of the fixed duration task

Fixed work

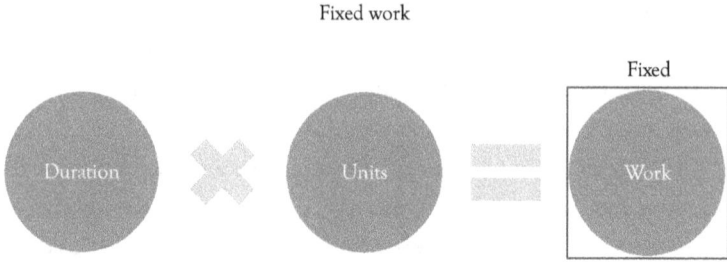

Figure 4.9 Conceptual view of fixed work task

Note

1 Chau (2007).

CHAPTER 5

Schedule Calculations

Objectives

On completion of this chapter, you should be able to

1. Understand the meaning and significance of critical path
2. Understand the meaning and significance of float
3. Use forward pass and backward pass to compute float
4. Use Resource leveling feature in MS-Project

Once a suitable network is drawn, with durations for all activities, the next step is to find out whether it meets the target completion date and what kind of flexibility exists in starting or ending these activities. In Chapter 3, we discussed about using different network diagrams for scheduling. In this chapter, we discuss how to arrive at the target completion date and how to find out the flexibility associated with starting or ending activities. We shall do this at two levels. First, we understand how to do calculations by hand, by using the precedence diagram. Then, we go ahead and discuss how to use MS-Project to do these computations. You may wonder why it is necessary to know how to do these manually. It is important to know how computations are done to fully understand the meaning of the float, early and late dates, and so on. Before going ahead with discussions related to schedule computations, let us understand the relevance of some terms (see Table 5.1).

Understanding Relevant Terms

Critical Path

Let us say that you have determined the activities, work packages, and dependencies. You have drawn the network diagram. The sponsor expects

Table 5.1 Schedule computation: Relevant terms

Critical Path: Critical path is the longest path through a project network. It, therefore, determines the earliest completion of the work.
Free Float: The amount of time an activity can be delayed without delaying the early start date of its successor.
Total Float: The amount of time an activity can be delayed without delaying the project completion date.
ES: Early start
LS: Late start
EF: Early finish
LF: Late finish

it to be finished within a specific duration. How do you find out whether it is feasible to finish within the duration with the help of the network diagram? Critical path helps you there. Once you complete the critical path analysis, you will also be able to determine the flexibility that exists in delaying some of these activities in the network. Let us look at the network diagram depicted in Figure 5.1. There are two network paths in the diagram. One is Start-A-B-C-E-End and the other is Start-A-D-E-End. The former is of 19 weeks' duration and the longer path. Hence, this is the critical path for the network.

Float, Forward Pass, and Backward Pass

Once you find out the critical path, you will also observe that you can delay the start date or end date of activities on a noncritical path to a limited extent, without affecting the start of the successor activity or the end date of the project. As we discussed in Table 5.1, the amount of time for

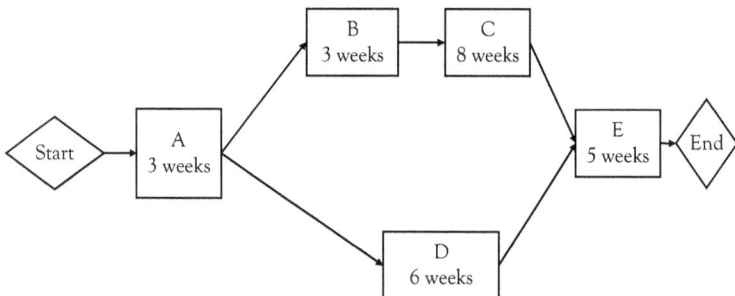

Figure 5.1 Sample network used for critical path computations

which you can delay an activity without delaying the start date of the successor is called free float and the amount of time for which you can delay an activity without delaying the project completion date is called total float. Total float is often known as slack and on a critical path slack is zero.

To go ahead with the computation of the total float associated with the activity, let us consider the network shown in Figure 5.1 again. The total float associated with an activity is the difference between the late start and the early start (or late finish and early finish) as mentioned in the illustration in Figure 5.2.

To complete hand calculations related to total float, the first step is to compute these terms. Let us again consider the sample network diagram discussed previously (Figure 5.1). Starting from A, compute the early start and early finish for the activities' upper path in the network diagram, that is, ABCE and note these on the top corners of each box (node), as shown in Figure 5.3. Similarly, do it for the path below, that is, activities ADE. This is called forward pass. It is important to look at where the paths converge in order to correctly perform the forward pass and the backward pass.

Keeping the earliest finish as the latest finish for the last activity in the network diagram, traverse backward to compute the latest finish and start dates for all activities. This is called backward pass. Here also, be careful at nodes where the backward computations converge (like A in this case).

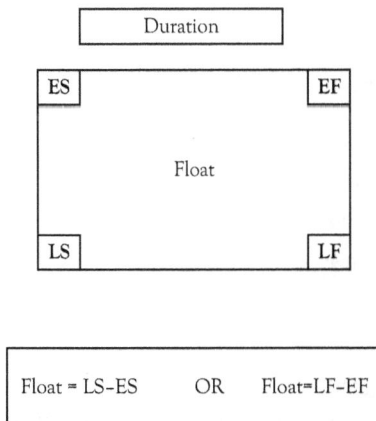

Figure 5.2. Float computation formulae for total float

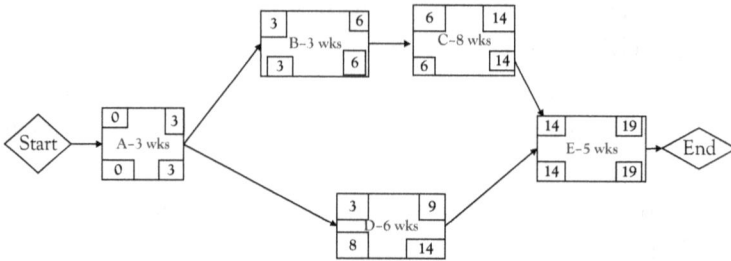

Figure 5.3 Forward and backward pass computations for the sample network

The path ABCE is critical path; therefore it will not have slack. Since ADE is noncritical path, it can have slack. Activity A and E are on the critical path; therefore they will not have slack. Only activity D can have total float. Slack for D is either (8–3) or (14–9), and is 5 weeks.

It is important that a project manager knows the critical path and float associated with the activities on the noncritical path. It allows for better allocation of resources. We shall discuss this in subsequent chapters.

Example Problem: Calculating Critical Path and Float

Let us consider a small project of Math Library Development, which has two modules. Note that activities are represented by tasks in MS-Project as there is no terminology called "Activity" in MS-Project.

Now let us see step by step how we can use MS-Project to find out the critical path and activity floats.

1. Copy sample project file **Math Lib-orginal.mpp** from the **Prac-tice-Files/Ch05** folder to your working folder and rename it as **Math Lib.mpp**. Double click and open the project file. The file will open as shown in Figure 5.4.

2. Next we identify the critical path using formatting. For that, first click on the **Projects** tab. Now click on the **Format** tab and, from the **Bar styles** group, click **Critical Path** check-box. The tasks (activities) on the critical path get highlighted in red (see gray task bars in Figure 5.5).

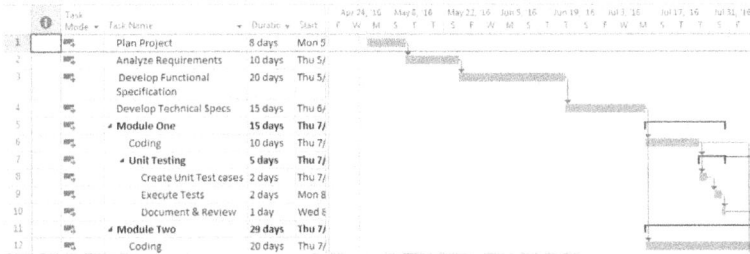

Figure 5.4 Gantt Chart for Math lib Project

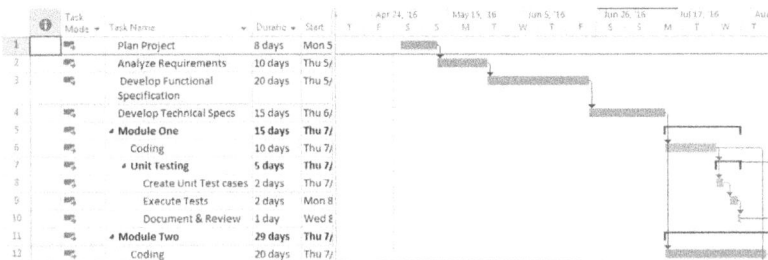

Figure 5.5 Critical path generated for the example file.

Note: Critical path gets highlighted in red (darker gray bars in picture)

3. However, you may be interested to see the network diagram. Select the **Task** tab. In the **View** group, click on the arrow, to change the view (and you get a pull-down menu with different views). Select **Network diagram**. You will see the network diagram as shown in Figure 5.6.

4. Again display the Gantt Chart view. To find out the float of each task (float is also known as slack), first click on the **Projects** tab. Next, select the **Format tab** and then click the **Slack** check-box from the **Bar Styles** group. Lines indicating slack get displayed. If you move the cursor on these lines, the corresponding slack information gets highlighted (Figure 5.7).

5. You can also insert a field indicating the slack. Double click on the title of any field in the table and select **Finish Slack** from the list displayed (you can start typing the word *Finish..*, to make your choice easier). Finish slack is the difference between the latest and earliest finishing dates of the task. Finish slack also gets displayed in the chart area. You may move the cursor on slack lines displayed in the

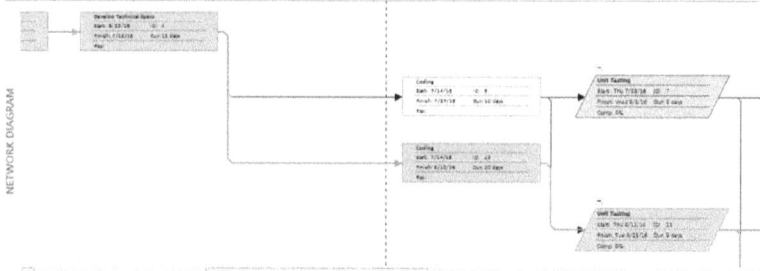

Figure 5.6 *Network view (partially displayed) for the example file*

Figure 5.7 *Slack (float) computed by MS-Project for each task*

chart area to get (flash) more information (Note: In this example, we demonstrate MS-Project features related to critical path and float, for a file without resources. However, in actual practice you will be doing this exercise for a resource loaded plan).

6. Close the file using the **File** tab. You may save the file with a suitable name like **Math lib_completed**.

Resource Leveling

As you plan the schedule, you may find that the demand for resources exceeds the maximum number of available resources at times (Figure 5.8). This requires coming out with a resource-limited schedule. Resource leveling can be done in three ways. There are three options for resource leveling:

- Delay the activity, use the float
- Increase resources
- Delay the project completion date

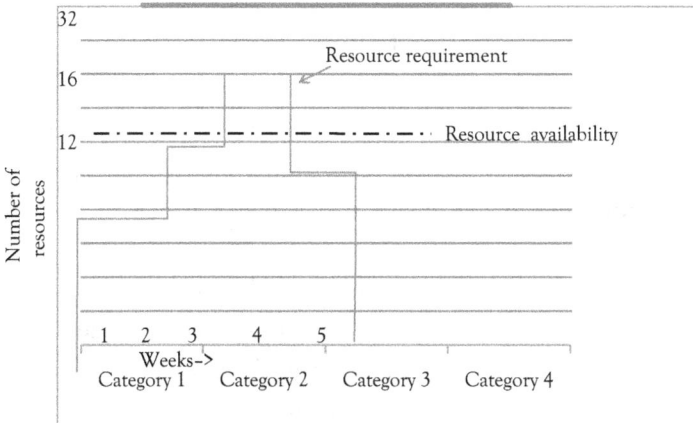

Figure 5.8 Without leveling, resource requirement may surpass the availability on some weeks

Example Problem: Resource Leveling Using MS-Project

Let us say you have to test three modules of software, as a part of your project. The project plan has already been prepared. You have to analyze the resource overloading and level resources using MS-Project. The following steps demonstrate the same.

1. Copy the file **Resource-level-Start.mpp** from the **Practice-Files/ Ch05** folder to your working directory and rename it as Resource-level. Open the project file **Resource-level.mpp** by double clicking on it. Observe the Gantt Chart. In case the file opens up with a different view, click on **View** tab **Task Views** group and click on the **Gantt Chart**. You will observe that the indicator column contains an indicator of a red person (also known as the *Burning Man* icon, indicating that the task has been assigned to overallocated resources)for tasks like *Study Test Plan* and *Execute Tests* subtasks (Figure 5.9).

2. Switch to Resource Sheet view. For this, click on the **Resource Sheet** button on the right-hand bottom of the screen. You will observe the project has two units of a resource called *Installer*. The Resource details are highlighted in red (Figure 5.10). If you move the cursor over the indicator, a message *The resource is over allocated* appears.

(Note: The default currency gets assigned in a project file based on the country in which you do the installation of MS-Project. However, the currency used in a project, say in case of Resource Rates can be changed. To do that click on the **File** tab and select **Options**. **Project Options** dialog appears. Select **Display** tab and in the **Currency Options** for the Project use the dropdown **Currency** to assign appropriate currency.)

3. The extent of resource overloading can be confirmed by using the Resource Graph view (Figure 5.11). For this, click on the **Resource** tab and select **Resource Graph** from the pull-down menu in the **Views** group. You will observe bars crossing Peak Units available and turning red as shown in Figure 5.11 (note that the graph you view may differ slightly from the one illustrated here in the chapter, based on the zoom factor and timescale).

4. Click on the **Views** tab, and in the **Task Views** group, click on the arrow of the **Gantt Chart** button and select **More Views.** From the **More Views** dialog that appears, select **Leveling Gantt and** click on **Apply.** Now you will find that task bars become thin and the file is ready for leveling. Although this step is not a must, it will help us to visualize the changes that would occur during leveling.

5. Now select the **Resource** tab. Click on **Level Resource** from the **Level** group. You will get the **Level Resource** dialog (Figure 5.12). Select the Resource *Tester* and click on **Level Now** button. MS-Project creates a resource-leveled schedule (Figure 5.13).

Note: You can set various options to control leveling using **Leveling Options** button in the **Level** group.

Although the project end date gets shifted to a later date, you find that the *Burning Man* icon has disappeared from the Gantt chart. You

Figure 5.9 Gantt Chart of the project before leveling

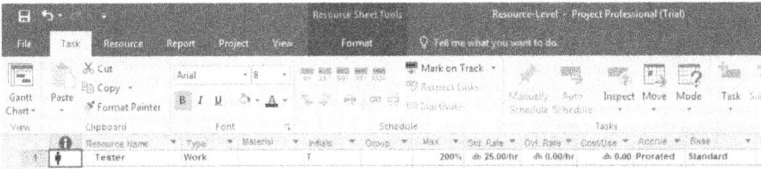

Figure 5.10 Resource Sheet of the project before leveling

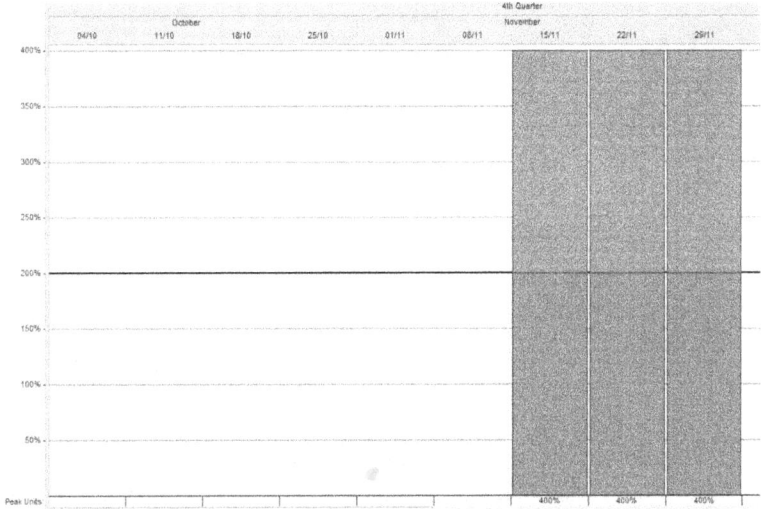

Figure 5.11 Resource Graph of the project before leveling

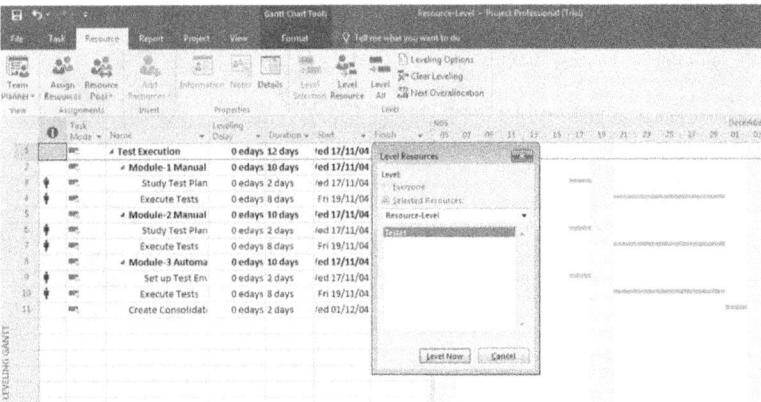

Figure 5.12 Use Level Resources dialog to select resources to be leveled in the leveling Gantt Chart

can go to the **Resource graph** view of the project plan again (as explained in earlier steps) and observe how the resource leveling has been achieved (Figure 5.14). Close the file.

To conclude, we discussed about the Critical path and Float as a part of schedule development in this chapter. At the end, we also saw an example of achieving resource-leveled schedule using MS-Project.

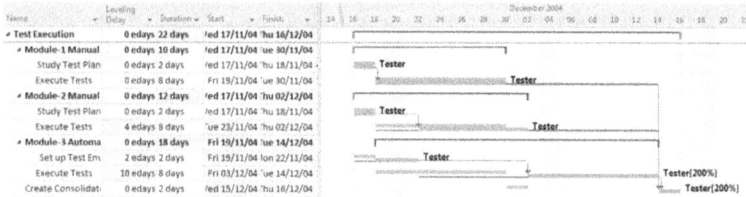

Figure 5.13 Tasks in the Gantt Chart, after leveling

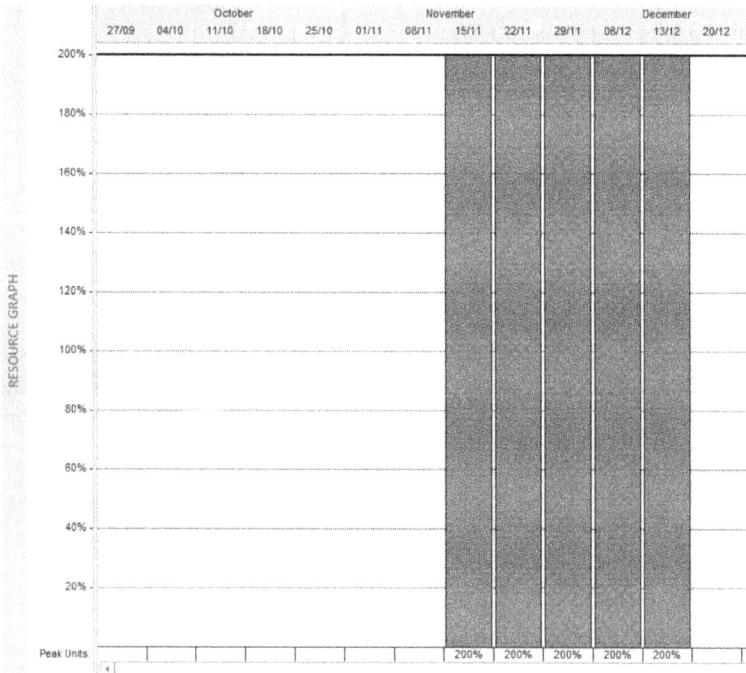

Figure 5.14 Resource graph after leveling

CHAPTER 6

Estimating Costs and Arriving at Budget

Objectives

On completion of this chapter, you should be able to understand

1. How to estimate the project budget
2. How to use MS-Project for estimating the project budget

Once you understand the scope of the work and plan the schedule, the next logical step is to arrive at the cost of tasks and computing the budget. In this chapter, we shall discuss key project management processes related to cost, namely, estimating and budgeting. Cost is a key constraint in most of the projects and it is important that the project is completed within the approved budget to keep the cost of the resultant product or service competitive.

Estimating costs is the process of approximating financial resources needed to complete the project activities (identified as tasks in MS-Project). The next step in arriving at the budget involves aggregating the estimated costs of individual activities or work packages and adding reserves (like contingency and management reserves), at appropriate stages. This will establish a cost baseline for the project. The *cost baseline* is the baseline of the project that gives us an idea about the amount of money the project is estimated to cost and how the money will be spent over a period of time (giving an idea of cash flow). Generally, it is an approved budget (by the sponsor) usually in a time-distribution format used to estimate, monitor, and control the overall cost performance of the project.

The Cost Tree Structure

To begin with, let us understand how we arrive at the project budget. Chapters 2 and 3 discussed about the work breakdown structure (WBS) and activity definitions. Figure 6.1 illustrates how individual activities are rolled up to form work packages. As a first step in estimating the cost of work packages, the work packages are decomposed into smaller components called activities. The activity definition process deals with creating activities (also known as schedule activities) by breaking down work packages. It is these activities that require cost estimation. This is known as the estimate costs process. Once these costs are estimated, contingency allowances are added to these estimates at various levels. Contingency reserves are allowances that a project manager will use, in case the identified risks get realized. These are then rolled up into associated work package costs. The same process is repeated at the work package

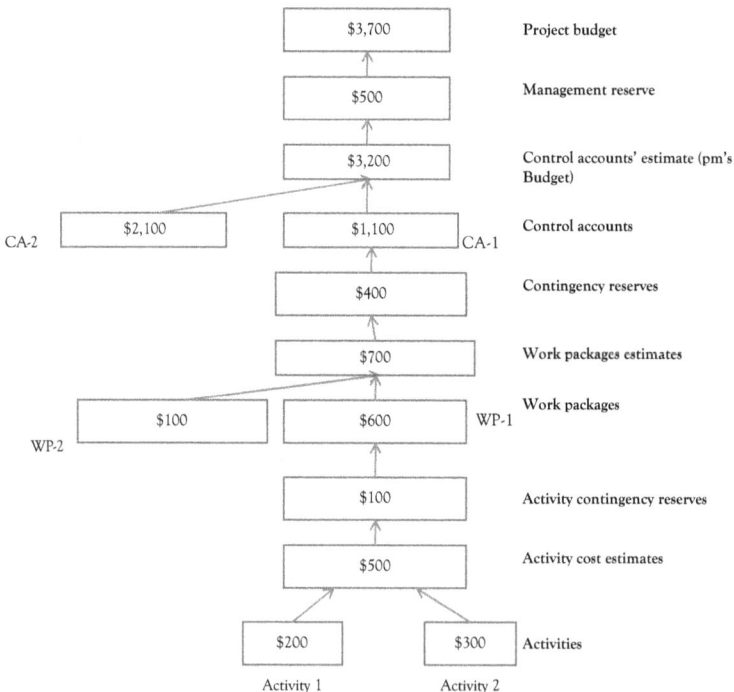

Figure 6.1 Estimating the project budget (WP stands for work packages and CA for control accounts)

level to come out with the control account estimates. (Control account is the WBS component used for the project cost accounting. Each control account is assigned a unique code to link it to the performing organization's accounting system.)

These control account estimates have to be rolled up and added with reserves. Management reserves are budgets that a project manager shall use with the approval of the senior management, to mitigate the effect of unplanned or unexpected changes to scope and cost. (As discussed earlier, in the case of MS-Project, we have only tasks to represent activities, work packages, control accounts, and so on. However, we can use subtasks to represent activities and summary tasks to represent work packages and control accounts, etc.)

With a basic understanding of how a budget is determined by rolling up costs, let us examine how MS-Project allows us to accomplish this. This case study deals with a small project of Software Testing.

Example Problem: Arriving at the Budget for a Software Testing Project

In the following example, we discuss the case of arriving at the budget of a small software testing project. The resources required and the quantities of the material have been estimated. Based on this, we shall estimate the cost of the project.

1. You need to use the project file named **Testing-project-with-resources-original.mpp** for this case study. Copy the file from the **Practice-Files/Ch06** folder to your working directory and rename as **Testing-project-with-resources**. Double click on the file. You will find a task list as illustrated in Figure 6.2. Click on the **Task** tab, and in the **View** group select **Gantt Chart** to go to the Gantt Chart view, if you do not see the task list.

    It is a project with two summary tasks (Planning & Preparation, Execute Tests).

2. Make the project summary task also visible, if required. For that, click on the **Format** tab and in the **show hide** group select **Summary Tasks** and **Project Summary Task** check-boxes.

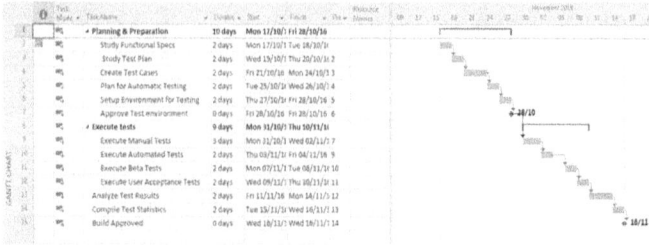

Figure 6.2 Gantt Chart of the software testing project

3. Now let us start estimating costs associated with each of the tasks. For that, resources have to be assigned to relevant tasks. Let us look at the Resource Sheet to start with. Click on the **View** tab and select **Resource Sheet** in the **Resource Views** group. You will see the resources associated with the project (Figure 6.3). These resources have associated costs too. Here are some points to be noted. The resource, *Licensed Software*, has got costs associated on the basis of its usage and has been categorized as a work resource. (If the license had been procured by outright purchase by one-time payment for this project, then it could have been categorized as a material resource.) Contingency allowances in this project are allocated to Execute Automated Tests, and are to be used in case the project needs support of an external consultant.

4. These resources have to be assigned to various tasks to estimate the costs associated with each task and thereby the baseline cost of the project. Switch to Gantt Chart (using **View** tab and **Task Views** group). Select the task *Planning & Preparation* from the **Resource** tab, **Assignments** group, select **Assign Resources**. The **Assign Resources** dialog pops up (Figure 6.4). You may keep this dialog open throughout the assignment process. There is no need to close the dialog, every time you select a different task.

Figure 6.3 Resource sheet of the software testing project

5. Select *QA Engineer* from the dialog. There is an option to change the units here and the cost of the work resources gets reflected accordingly in the next column. In this case, *QA Engineer* is working full time on this task and hence we need to apply 100 percent. (By default, 100 percent gets assigned in case of work resources, when you use assign button. You need not exclusively specify the same.)

6. Now repeat the previous step for the rest of the tasks according to Table 6.1 without closing the **Assign Resources** dialog. When you assign additional resources like Hardware, you get an *Action button* in the *Task Mode* column. Accept the default option is "Increase the amount of work but keep the duration same" as there is no need to change.

   With this you have assigned all the required resources to all the tasks. As you observe, the contingency allowance of $620 has been assigned to the task *Execute Automated Tests*. This may be used to hire an expert or consultant to guide the staff in the usage of the tool.

7. As a last step, let us analyze the estimated costs. Now we have the resources displayed with the bar charts. However, we will still not get an idea about costs associated with work packages and so on, and the project as a whole. To have an idea about the same we have to add a Cost column. For that, move the separator between the chart and the table toward left-hand side. An additional new column gets

Table 6.1 Resources assignment details for the project

Tasks	Resources	Units/cost
Planning and Preparation (Summary Task)	QA Engineer Hardware	100% 100%
Study Functional Specifications	Project Manager	50%
Execute Tests (Summary Task)	Hardware QA Engineer	100% 100%
Execute Automated Tests	Licensed Software Contingency Allowance	100% U.S. $ 620
Execute User Acceptance Tests	Travel	U.S. $2,100
Analyze Test Results	Project Manager QA Engineer	100% 100%
Compile Test Statistics	QA Engineer Paper	100% 2 Rims

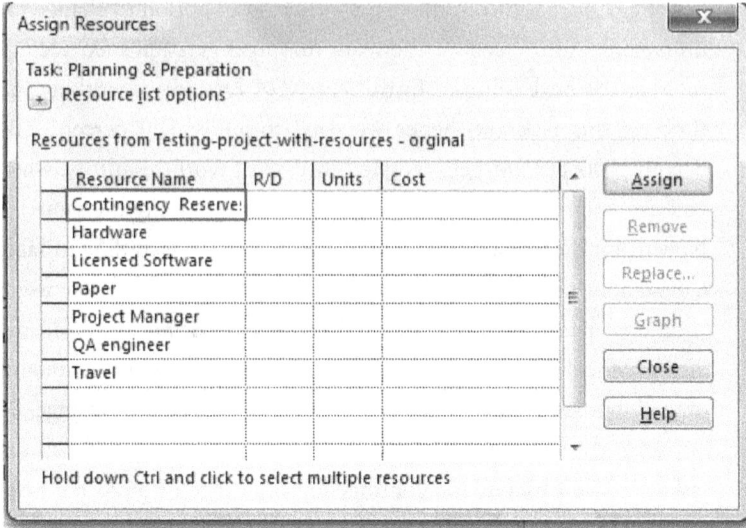

Figure 6.4 Assign resources dialog box

displayed with the title *Add new column*. Click on the arrow there and select **Cost** from the pull-down list. The **Cost** column gets displayed. The rolled-up costs are displayed too for the project (Figure 6.5). As you notice some of the subtasks like "Study Test Plan" are displayed with zero cost though they use resources like "Hardware," as those costs are covered (or accounted) by their summary tasks. Close the **Testing-project-with-resources** file.

To conclude, we did learn how to arrive at the project budget summing up various costs and allowances, in this chapter. We also did study, with an example, how we can initiate the process of estimating the project budget with the help of MS-Project.

Figure 6.5 Display the rolled-up costs to display the estimated budget

CHAPTER 7

Tracking Project

Objectives

On completion of this chapter, you should be able to

1. Understand how to set a baseline
2. Understand how to set the status date and the current date
3. Understand how to record progress of various tasks during project execution
4. Understand what is meant by earned value (EV)
5. Understand how MS-Project can be used to compute the EV metrics

In previous chapters, we discussed the use of Microsoft Project Professional, for project planning. Many a professional and organization limit the use of the software just for that. However, MS-Project can also be used to update the progress made. This is very important, considering that this will help us use MS-Project throughout the project life cycle. After updating the tasks with the progress made, we can do earned value analysis (EVA), to compute important parameter indices like Schedule Variance, Cost Variance, Cost Performance Index, and Schedule Performance Index. In this chapter, we shall discuss how Microsoft Project Professional can be used for tracking projects and doing EVA, to analyze project performance. We will also study about various formulas related to EVA, with simple examples.

Establishing a Baseline and Updating the Schedule

We can update the tasks with percentage completion information, and actual start and end dates, to reflect the actual status of projects. We need a file to do this and we use the file **enhancement-start.mpp**. Copy the file from the **Practice-Files/Ch07** folder to your working directory and rename it as **enhancement.mpp.**

1. Double click the file and have a look at the tasks, in the Gantt Chart view (Figure 7.1).

   To start with project tracking, we need to prepare the file and the following are a few steps to be followed for the same.

2. In the **View** tab, select **Tracking Gantt** from the pull-down menu on the left-hand side. Tracking Gantt view will be shown. You will now have thin bars representing tasks as shown in Figure 7.2. The bars also turn red as the Critical Path gets highlighted in red. All bars become red in this case, as all tasks are on the Critical Path.

3. The next step is setting a baseline. Baseline is like a snapshot and provides a basis for comparison. To set a baseline, select the **Project** tab. From the **Schedule** group, click **set baseline** and select **set baseline**.

   Set Baseline dialog will appear, as shown in Figure 7.3. Accept all default values and set the baseline for the Entire Project. You can set

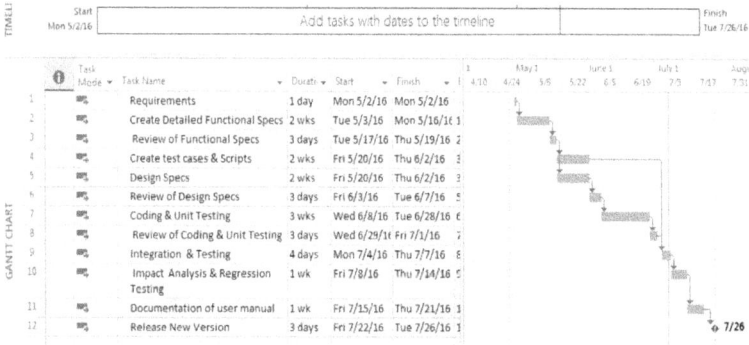

Figure 7.1 Gantt chart of the software enhancement project

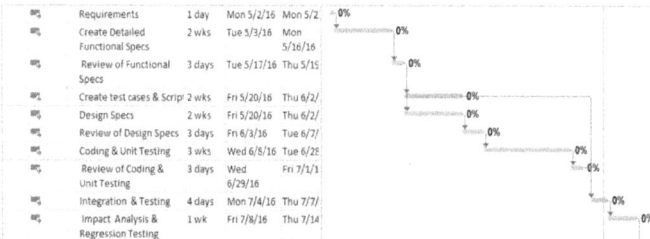

Figure 7.2 Tracking Gantt chart of the project

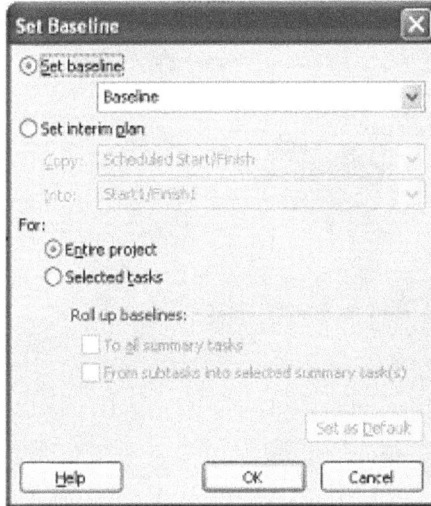

Figure 7.3 Set baseline dialog box

11 baselines in MS-Project. The baseline bars will be shown in gray, along with bars showing planned values.

Next we define the status date using Project Information Dialog. In the **Project** tab, Properties group, click on **Project Information** button. The Project Information dialog box appears, as shown in Figure 7.4. As you all know, in any project, it takes time to get progress information to us, as data may have to be gathered from a remote project site. The **Status Date** setting allows us to enter the date/time when the data are valid. Let us say that we have the status of the tasks that were completed as effective at **17:00** on Friday, **May 20th, 2016.** We need to set this up through the **Project Information** dialog. Select using the calendar pick or enter using the keyboard, the **Status Date.** The **Status Date** assumes a default point in time of **17:00.**

4. Now we are ready to feed the actual task or project information. Let us say, in this case information has come in that task Requirements was delayed by a day. We need to feed that into our schedule. Select the task *Requirements* in the Gantt Chart view.

5. In the **Task** tab, in the **Schedule** group, click the arrow next to **Mark on Track** and select **Update Tasks** (Figure 7.5). **Update Tasks** Dialog

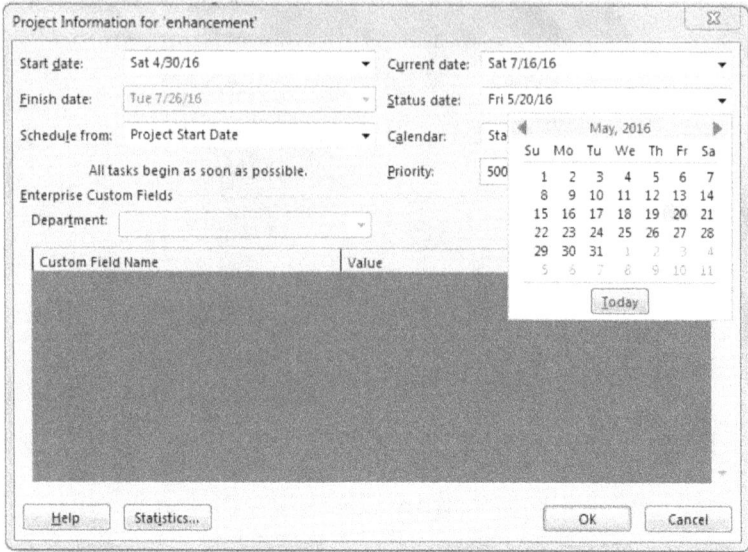

Figure 7.4 Use project information dialog box to define status date,
current date and so on.

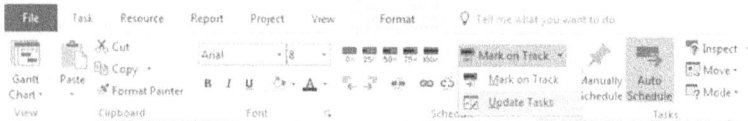

Figure 7.5 Select "Update Tasks from Mark on Track," to update the
actual start date, and so on.

appears. Mention the actual start date in the appropriate format or
use the calendar pick list to select the start date. The task bar of the
first task shifts now, along with dependent tasks. Baseline schedule
will also be juxtaposed, making the comparison easier.

Next we shall update tasks with percentage completion. For
this, click on the task that you want to update in the Gantt Chart.
To start with, select the task *Requirements* and from Task tab and
the **Schedule** group, click **100 percent**. The bars will get filled and
100 percent will be displayed near the task bar, in the Gantt Chart
view. Like this, update 75 percent completion, for the task *Create
Detailed Functional Specs.* (Note that you can easily segregate incom-
plete tasks as the indicator column gets ticked as tasks are updated to
100 percent completion as shown in Figure 7.6)

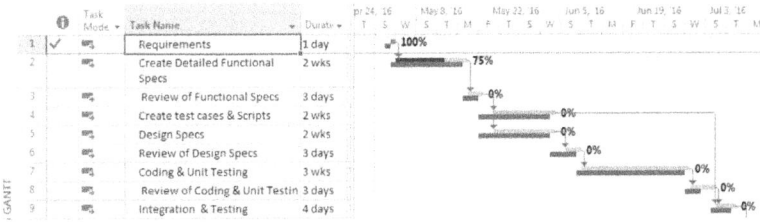

Figure 7.6 *Use percentage completion buttons from task tab and schedule group to update the progress*

With this we complete updating the tasks in the Tracking Gantt view. Observing the same will give one the idea about the project progress. Save the file and close the session.

Earned Value Analysis

Earned value management (EVM) is a commonly used method of performance measurement and is applied to all projects, across all industry sectors. It gives a three-dimensional view of the project progress as it integrates project scope, cost, and schedule measures and can be used to monitor the progress for the entire duration of the project. EVM can be used to manage schedule performance bonus of contractors, and also to drive invoicing in projects.

Understanding Key Terms and EV Metrics

Some key definitions that would help you go ahead with EV computations are presented in Table 7.1.

Table 7.1 *Key terms for EV computations*

Term	Abbreviation	Definition
Planned value	PV	It is the approved budget assigned to the work that has to be accomplished (also known as performance measurement baseline)
Earned value	EV	It is the value of the work performed
Actual cost	AC	It is the cost actually incurred in performing the work (for which EV is measured)

Table 7.2 EV Four important metrics

Term	Abbreviation	Definition
Schedule variance	SV	It is a measure of schedule performance of the project. It can indicate whether a project is behind or ahead of schedule. It is the difference between EV and planned value. It is computed using the formula SV = EV − PV.
Cost variance	CV	It is a measure of cost performance of the project. It can indicate whether a project is under the budget or over the budget. It is the difference between EV and actual cost. It is computed using the formula CV = EV − AC.
Schedule Performance Index	SPI	It is a ratio of progress achieved to progress planned and is computed by the formula SPI = EV/PV. If it is more than 1, then it means more work is completed than was planned.
Cost Performance Index	CPI	It is a ratio of the value of the work completed to the actual cost and is computed by formula CPI = EV/AC. If it is more than 1, then it means that project has cost under run.

Based on these three values, we compute four important metrics that enable us to measure the performance of the project. Those four are explained in Table 7.2.

A Simple Example of EV

To understand this better let us take a simple example of doing an enhancement. Let us say, you have to build **4** modules in four days (at the rate 1 module/day), as shown in Figure 7.7. Let us say the cost of building the same is estimated to be U.S. $100 per module.

Planned: 4 modules in 4 days

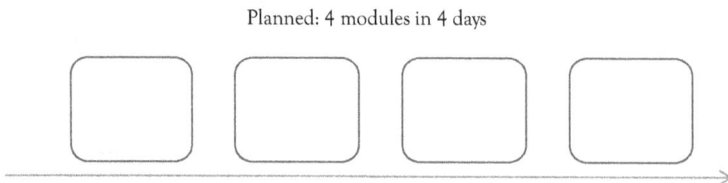

Figure 7.7 Planned work that is worth U.S. $400

Status: 3 modules in 4 days

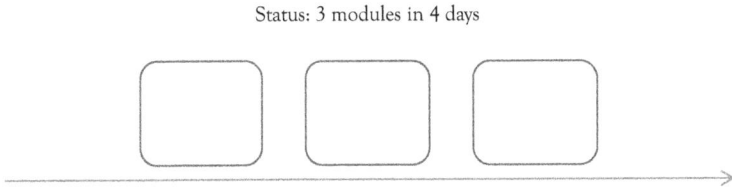

Figure 7.8 Completed work worth of $300 (after four days)

After four days, you monitor the work done and find that only 3 Modules has been built instead of 4 modules. That means PV was $400. EV is only $300 (Figure 7.8). As far as the schedule is concerned, you are lagging. However, you find that only $200 was spent for the work done. This means that the cost variance is $100, which is positive and good, as it ascertains that you have spent less.

Similarly, we can also compute CPI and SPI.

CPI = EV/AC = 300/200 = 1.5

This means that for every $1 you spend, you are getting 1.5 times worth of work done.

SPI = EV/PV = 300/400 = 0.75

This means that the work is getting done at 75 percent of the planned rate.

Forecasting

Forecasting is a technique of making predictions based on the available information. As the project progresses, the project management team can develop a forecast for estimate at completion (EAC) based on the past performance. Table 7.3 gives a quick look at the terms.

There are three common methods to arrive at EAC. These are based on various scenarios.

1. Assuming that all the future ETC work will be accomplished at the budgeted rate:

   EAC = AC + BAC – EV

2. Assuming that the remaining work will be performed at the same CPI:

Table 7.3 Forecasting: four important terms

Term	Abbreviation	What it means?
Estimate at completion	EAC	How much do we expect the total project to cost (based on the current information)?
Estimate to complete	ETC	How much more do we expect it to cost to finish the project?
Budget at completion	BAC	What is the amount that we had budgeted for the project effort in to?
Variance at completion	VAC	By how much we will exceed (either positive or negative) the budget when we finish the project?

$$EAC = BAC/(Cumulative\ CPI)$$

3. Assuming that the work will be done with same CPI and SPI

$$EAC = AC + (BAC - EV)/(Cumulative\ CPI \times Cumulative\ SPI)$$

The **To Complete Performance Index (TCPI)** is the calculated projection of cost performance that must be achieved on the remaining work to meet a specific management goal (this may be either BAC or EAC). Let us say that as a Project Manager, you have prepared a new EAC and it is approved, then the TCPI based on the new EAC is computed using formula

$$TCPI = (BAC - EV)/(EAC - AC)$$

EVA Using MS-Project

Now that we know the definition or meaning of various indices like SPI (Schedule Performance Index), let us see how MS-Project can be used for EVM, variance analysis, and so on. For this purpose, we shall do an exercise, hands-on, using MS-Project.

1. Copy the file **web-site-improvement-start.mpp** from **Practice-Files/ Ch07** to your working directory and rename as **web-site-improve-ment.mpp**.
2. Double click on the file **web-site-improvement.mpp** from the files folder. By looking at the Gantt Chart, you will observe that it is a

simple project with only two tasks (Figure 7.9). Both tasks will start on August 23rd, 2016

3. Go to the Resource Sheet view and observe the existing resources of the project. Two Resources, Dave and Sunny are working on the project (Figure 7.10). Dave has a standard rate of 12 Euros/hour and Sunny has a standard rate of 8 Euros/ hr.

   Dave and Sunny will work a maximum of 8 hour a day.

   As we are ready with tasks and Resource Sheet, we can assign different resources to different tasks. In this case, please do note that the estimated total duration to complete the project is 10 days and the estimated work for each task (UI improvement and Performance Tuning) is 80 hr. Let us assign Dave to UI Improvement and Sunny to Performance Tuning. (Click on Resource Tab and in the Assignments Group, select Assign Resources to start doing the same.) With this the project plan is ready.

4. On **Project** tab and **Schedule** group, click **Set Baseline** button **and** select **Set Baseline**. Set Baseline dialog box appears. Check that the name of the baseline is *Baseline* in the (set baseline) the dialog box. Press **OK** to save the Baseline. (Note: You can verify the baseline information on the Project Statistics window. Select **Project** tab and then **Project Information** from **Properties** group. In the dialog box that appears click **Statistics.**)

5. The next step is tracking and updating the project plan. Let us say Dave and Sunny have started working on the project and you get reports on the weekends about the work done. Now you have to

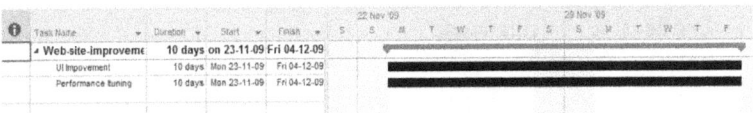

Figure 7.9 Gantt chart of the project plan with two tasks

Figure 7.10 Resource sheet of the project with just two resources

track the progress by feeding the data of the actual work in the Resource Usage Sheet and set the status date to enable EV-related computations. Let us say you have got the actual work-related information as in Table 7.4.

Although there are different methods, we are choosing Resource Usage view to update with (insert) the actual hours in the project plan.

On the **Resource** tab, in the **Resource Views** group, click on **Resource Usage** view. You get the Resource-Usage view with information of about the usage of resources on different tasks different days. Now check whether Actual work is listed below the work under each user's name. If it is not, then right click in the **Details** column. You get a **Detail-Styles** pop-up window, in which you can select **Actual-work** check-box and also Enter the Actual hours against the task. Click on the **File** tab and **Save** the project.

6. Status date has to be set for EV computation. Status date is the date when you last updated the project progress. It may be the current date, a date in the past, or a date in the future. To set the status date, click on the **Project** tab and **Project Information** from **Properties** group. In the dialog box that appears, change the Status Date to 11/27/09.

7. EV calculations are also based on the following settings in MS-Project.
   • Baseline Number
   • EV Calculation Method
   Baseline Number: If you have multiple baselines saved for your project, you have an option to specify which baseline you want to consider for EV calculations. In this example, we are using the very first baseline *Baseline* (the date on which it was saved is mentioned beside it) for calculations.

Table 7.4 Actual work information of the example

Resource	Work done between November 23rd, 2009 and Novemeber 27th, 2009 (hour/day)	Total actual work done (hour)
Dave	6	30
Sunny	8	40

EV Calculation Method: To get the accurate EV numbers, you need to specify the EV calculation methods in MS-Project Plan. EV calculations are always based on percent Complete or Physical percent Complete.

Now you have to set the aforementioned parameters using MS-Project options. For that, click **File,** select **Options,** and go to **Advanced.** In **EV Options for this project** (select the project name *web-site-improvement*), choose **Default task EV method as % complete** and **Baseline for EV calculations** from the drop-down menu as *Baseline* (Figure 7.11) click **OK** to close the **Project Options** dialog box. Save the project.

8. For EV-related computations, we have to apply EV Table to Tracking-Gantt. Select the **View** tab and from **Task Views** group **Tracking Gantt.** Right click on the left-hand side top corner of the table (below the Ribbon) and from the context/shortcut menu select **More Tables** and from the dialog box that appears, select **Earned Value** and then click **Apply.** In the right-most column in the table, click on the **Add new column** title type *TCPI.*

You will be viewing Tracking-Gantt with bars showing the actual progress beside the baseline schedule. EV analysis values will also be displayed (Figure 7.12).

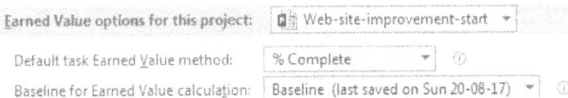

Figure 7.11 Set suitable Earned Value options for the project

Figure 7.12 Apply EV table to the project to compute the EVA metrics

Verifying the Computations

We can analyze the EV computed by MS-Project using the formulas discussed in earlier sections. We can verify whatever values we obtained using MS-Project match with the values we compute using the formulas.[1] The following steps elaborate the same.

Percentage Complete

(a) Percentage complete : 44.4 percent

Percentage complete is always related to duration. UI Improvement task was originally scheduled to be completed in 10 days. Due to less actual hours done for this task by Dave, now this task requires 11.25 days to complete. Out of the 11.25 days, the task had been completed in 5 days' duration. It means 44.4 percent of the task had been completed till now. That is $5 \times 100/11.25 = 44.4$ percent

(b) Percent complete of Performance Tuning task: 50 percent

Performance tuning task was originally scheduled to be completed in 10 days. Out of the 10 days' duration, the task had been completed at 5 days' duration. It means 50 percent of the task has been completed till now.

Percentage Work Complete

(a) Percent work complete of UI Improvement task: 37.5 percent

Original estimation is 80 hour of work. Out of 80 hour of planned work, 30 hour of task is actually completed. That is $100 \times 30/80 = 37.5$ percent.

(b) Percent work complete of Performance Tuning task: 50 percent

Original estimation is 80 hour of work. Out of the 80 hour of planned work, 40 hour of task is actually completed. That is 50 percent.

Baseline Cost or BAC

The Baseline Cost fields show the total planned cost for a task, a resource for all assigned tasks, or for work to be performed by a resource on a task. Baseline cost is also referred to as budget at completion (BAC), an EV field.

BAC for UI Improvement task is €960 (i.e., total 80 hour of the task was planned at the rate of €12)

BAC for Performance Tuning task is €640 (i.e., total 80 hour of the task was planned at the rate of €8)

BAC for the project plan is the total cost of UI Improvement and Performance Tuning tasks: €1,600

Planned Value

PV is also known as BCWS (budgeted cost of work scheduled). PV fields contain the cumulative time-phased baseline costs up to the status date or today's date.

PV for UI Improvement task:

> Status date of the project: 11/27/2009
>
> Planned hours (budgeted hours) for UI Improvement task till 11/27//2009: 40 hour resource assigned to UI Improvement task: Dave
>
> Dave's hourly rate: €12
>
> Planned cost (budgeted cost) for UI Improvement task till 11/27/2009: 40 × 12 = €480

PV for Performance Tuning task:

> Status date of the project: 11/27/2009
>
> Planned hours (budgeted hours) for Performance Tuning task till 11/27/2009: 40 hour resource assigned to Performance Tuning task: Sunny
>
> Sunny hourly rate: €8
>
> Planned cost (budgeted cost) for Performance Tuning task till 11/27/2009: 40 × 8 = €320
>
> BCWS for the project is €800 (i.e., €480 + €320)

Actual Cost

On similar lines (i.e., similar to PV), the actual cost for the project can be computed as (30 × 12 + 40 × 8) = €680

Earned Value

On similar lines, EV can be computed

EV of UI Improvement = €960 × Percentage complete of UI Improvement = €960 × 44.444/100 = 426.6

EV of Performance Tuning = €640 × Percentage complete of Performance Tuning = €640 × 50/100 = €320

EV for the project = €426.6 + €320 = €746.6

Using various formulas discussed in earlier sections and using the values of PV, EV, and AC we can compute CPI, SPI, CV, SV and so on, and verify the values (computed by MS-Project software) displayed in EV tables.

Save the file and close the session (using **File** tab).

To summarize in this chapter, we studied how MS-Project can be used to track a project and also to do an Earned Value Analysis (EVA). We also verified the computations done using

Note

1   Samant (2010).

CHAPTER 8

Reports

Objectives

On completion of this chapter, you should be able to

1. Understand the types and relevance of various reports in software projects
2. Understand various reports available in MS-Project
3. Learn how we can generate and customize reports native to MS-Project

Once the baseline of a project gets set and the project execution begins the primary focus of the project manager shifts to collecting, updating, analyzing, and disseminating project information. The project status–related information has to be communicated to various project stakeholders like customers and sponsors in a project. This shall help various stakeholders to monitor and control various project tasks.

Software projects can fail for many a reason. One of the reasons can be a lack of good communication during project execution. Project reports are used to communicate the status of a project to various stakeholders. A good project-reporting system facilitates effective management decision making and also provides the ability to drill down by layer. Here is a list of important project reports that are used in big information technology projects.

1. *Project Dashboard Report*: Contains project metrics represented on a single page. It presents quick, meaningful, and actionable information.

2. *Summary Management Report*: These are prepared monthly or fortnightly and summarize the cost- and work-related information, quality issues, and so on.

3. *Summary Cost Report*: Prepared by consolidating cost data from several sources. It is the most challenging task to prepare this report.

4. *Milestone and Upcoming Tasks (look ahead report)*: The milestone report helps us to understand the project status quickly and the look-ahead report gives project managers information about upcoming activities.

MS-Project Professional facilitates you to generate various reports. These can be broadly classified into two categories. One category of reports is Visual reports, which is supported by MS-Excel and MS-Visio. The other category (which has been added in the recent past) is to generate reports that are native to MS-Project. We will not discuss much about the generation of reports in MS-Excel and MS-Visio in this chapter. The

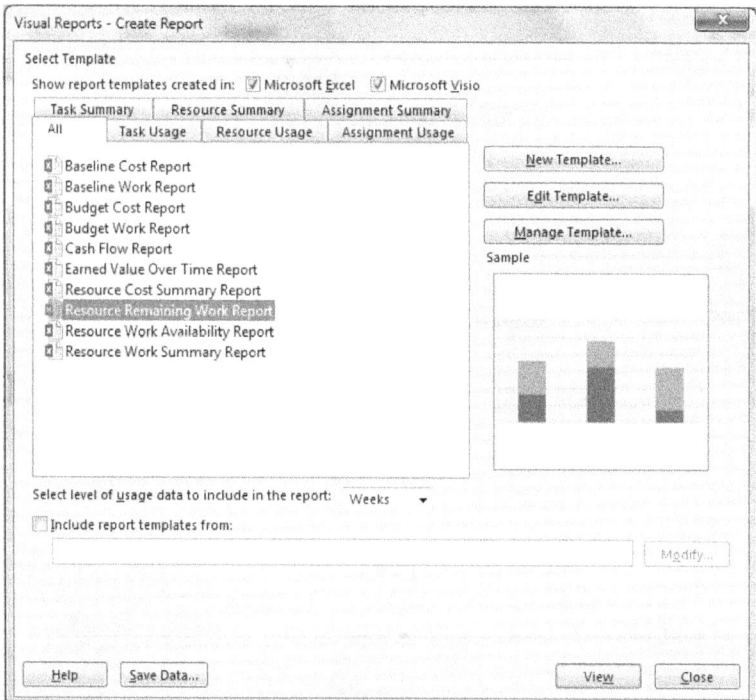

Figure 8.1 Use visual reports dialog to select the required reports

Resource Remaining Work Report

■ Actual Work   ▣ Remaining Work

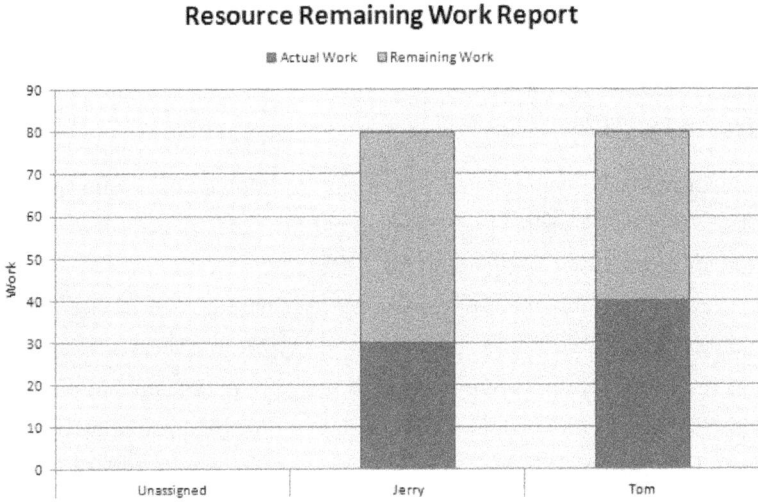

Figure 8.2 An example of visual report

discussion will be much focused on native reports of MS-Project. To generate Visual reports in MS-Excel or Visio, click on the **Report** Tab and Select **Visual Reports** from the **Export** Group. This will bring up the **Visual Reports** dialog, which can be used to select various reports, using check-boxes and different tabs as shown in Figure 8.1. When you click **View** in the dialog, an OLAP (Online Analytical Processing) cube file gets built and results are displayed in MS-Excel Pivot-chart or MS-Visio Pivot-table as shown in Figure 8.2. All such reports have been listed for your reference in Table 8.1.

Table 8.1 Various visual reports available in MS-Project

Microsoft Excel	Microsoft Visio (available in metric and US units)
Baseline cost report	Baseline report
Baseline work report	Critical task status report
Budget cost report	Cash flow report
Budget work report	Resource availability report
Cash flow report	Resource status report
Earned value over time report	Task status report
Resource cost summary report	
Resource remaining work report	
Resource work availability report	
Resource work summary report	

Example Problem: Generating Native Reports and Customizing Reports

Generating Native Reports

Generating native reports does not require additional office software like MS-Excel or MS-Visio. It uses readymade templates to generate reports related to resources, costs, and so on.

Let us consider the example project that we used for earned value analysis. We have two tasks: *UI Design* and *DB Design*. The work done by two resources has been recorded. Let us see how we can generate various reports and customize reports in this chapter. For this, you copy **bank_app_desn_complete.mpp** from the **Practice-Files/Ch08** folder to your working directory.

1. In MS-Project 2016, Click on the **File** Tab. Select Open and then click on the **Computer** and select **bank_app_desn_complete.mpp** from the appropriate (your working) folder. The file will open in MS-Project, showing two tasks in the Gantt Chart.
2. From the **Reports** tab, **View Reports** group, click **Dashboards**. From the pull-down menu, select **Project Overview** and you will get the project overview report, with bars indicating percentage completion as shown in Figure 8.3.

This is an example of Dashboard report, which is generated at the click of the mouse.

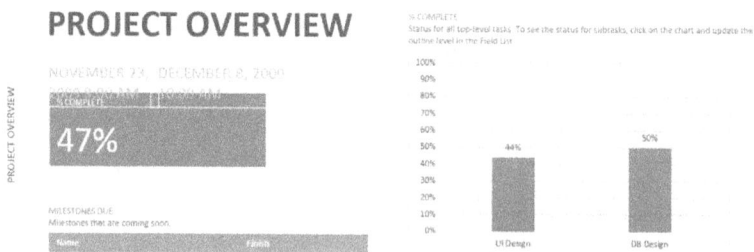

Figure 8.3 Project overview report: An example of dashboard report

Generating a Custom Report

We can customize available reports. However, in many situations, we may have to generate a customized report that has a mix of different data elements, charts, and tables. For this, we will continue working with the earlier example file **bank_app_desn_complete.mpp**.

1. On the **Report** tab, in the **View Reports** group, click **New Report**. Select **Blank** to start with a blank report. (You may display Entry Table in the Gantt Chart if required.)
2. In the Report Name dialog box that appears, enter the name that should be displayed as title at the top of the report. Enter *consolidated-cost-report* (Figure 8.4). Later on, you may access the customized report using **Report** tab, **View Reports** Group, **Custom** menu.
3. At first, you will add a chart to the report. One interesting way to express the cost of this plan is a pie chart, with each task (like *UI Design* and *DB Design*) of the plan represented as a slice of the pie chart. In a large project, it can be a summary task or phase, which may be of interest. You will label each slice of the pie chart with details like the name, cost, and percentage of the total cost for further clarification. This gives you a view of the project cost breakup.

   On the **Report Tools Design** tab, in the **Insert** group, click **Chart**. The **Insert Chart** dialog box appears (see Figure 8.5). Click and select **Pie** from various charts available like Bar, Line. Click **OK** to add a pie chart.
4. You will observe that the default pie chart does not contain the values you need. You will have to change those using the Field List pane displayed (on the right-hand side). Click on the pie chart if the pane is not displayed. In the **Field List** pane, in the **Select Fields** box, click the expand/

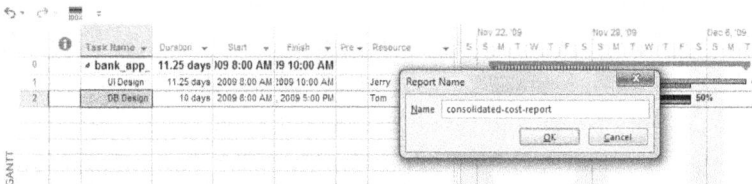

Figure 8.4 Enter a title for your customized report

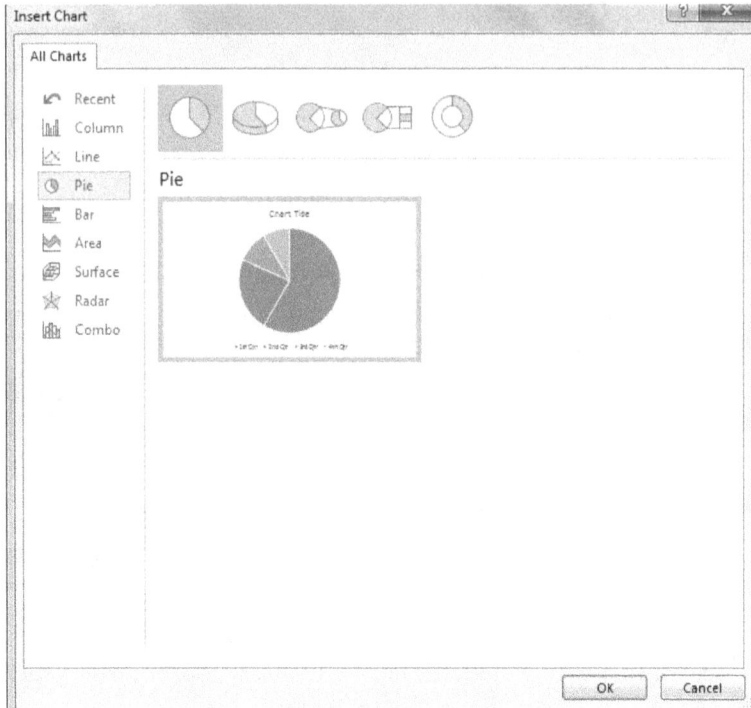

Figure 8.5 Select a chart type and add it to the report

collapse arrow next to **Cost** to expand the **Cost** field list, and then under **Custom**, select the **Cost** check-box. In the **Select Fields** box, under the **Work** fields list, under **Baseline**, clear (deselect) the **Work** check-box (as you do not want this field). You can also clear other work-related fields (say, e.g., **Remaining Work**) that you do not want. You will see a pie chart representing the costs of the two tasks (Figure 8.6).

5. Now add data labels to the slices. (If the Chart Tools tabs are not visible, click on the pie chart.) On the **Chart Tools Design** tab, in the **Chart Layouts** group, click **Add Chart Element**, point to **Data Labels**, and then click **More Data Label Options**.

The Format Data Labels pane appears on the right-hand side as shown in Figure 8.7 (ignore the Field List pane for now). Select Category Names and Percentage using the appropriate check-boxes (and leave other check-boxes as they are). Category names of slices appear. Close the Format Data Labels pane.

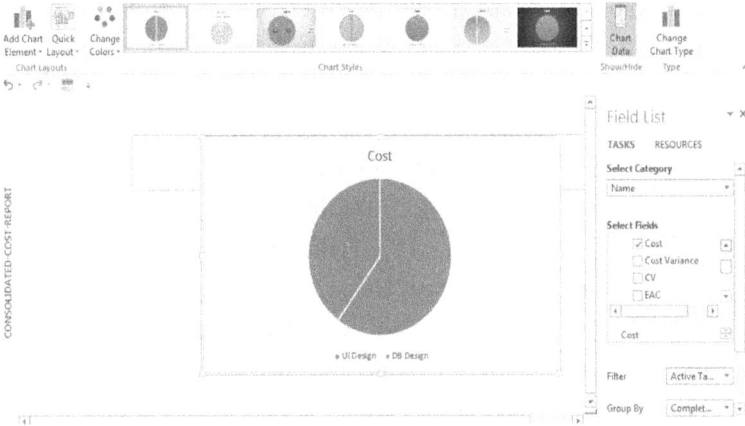

Figure 8.6 Add relevant fields to display the values in the default pie chart

6. Now that the Data Labels are visible and Legends are not necessary any more. You may hide the same. For that, on the **Chart Tools Design** tab, in the **Chart Layouts** group, click **Add Chart Element**, point to **Legend**, and then click **None**.

7. Next you will be adding a table below the chart to reflect CPI (Cost Performance Index, discussed in earlier chapters) and also the cost of the task. Initially, you will add the table with the default fields. For that, click anywhere outside of the chart to deselect it. On the **Report Tools Design** tab, in the **Insert** group, click **Table**. Drag the table below the pie chart (by using the cursor and holding the border) once added.

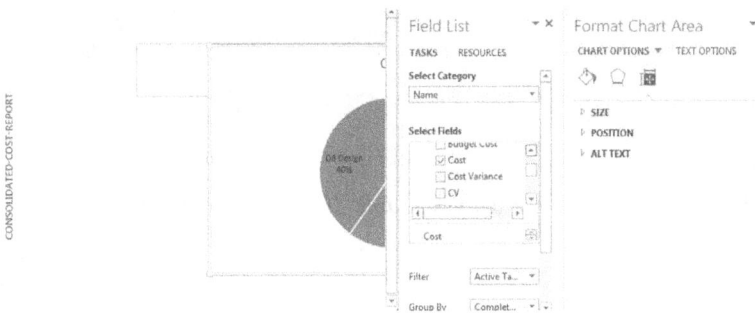

Figure 8.7 Use Format Data Labels pane to pick, position, and format required data labels suitably

8. The table may not contain the task list (even the top-level summary tasks). Two tasks, Wall A and Wall B, have to be added. Click on the table and view the Field List Pane on the right-hand side). For that, at the **Outline Level** (on the lower side of the **Field List Pane**) use the pull-down menu and add **Level 1**.

9. You have to add the two fields for the table and remove fields that are not required. For that, in the **Field List Pane,** click on the arrow mark **Date** and Expand **Date.** Under **Custom** clear **Start** and **Finish.** Expand **Cost** and then **Custom** and select **Cost.** Similarly, expand the **Number** and select **Custom** and then **CPI.** You may have to clear fields like **Percent Complete** by selecting **Custom** under **Number** if required. With this, you have completed customizing the table (Figure 8.8). Close the **Field List** Pane and **save** the file.

10. Now you see that, under **Reports** tab, **View Reports** group, when you click the **Custom**, the *consolidated-cost-report* is available. **Close** the project file.

To conclude, we did take a quick look at various reports that are relevant to Information Technology projects and also the available visual reports in MS-Project. Through a guided example, we studied how to customize native reports in MS-Project.

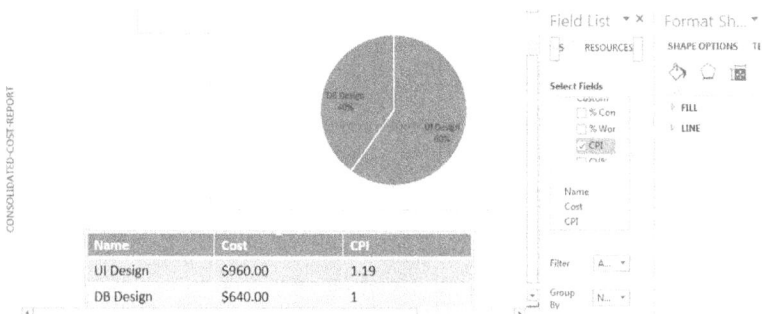

Figure 8.8 Add a table with cost and CPI fields, to the custom report using the Field List Pane

CHAPTER 9

Managing Multiple Projects

Objectives

On completion of this chapter, you should be able to

1. Understand what is meant by an external dependency in a project
2. Understand how to represent external dependency in an MS-Project schedule
3. Understand the concept of master project and subproject
4. Understand different ways of merging subprojects
5. Understand the creation and use of resource pool

In earlier chapters, we discussed about managing a single project. However, a project may be very big, and may have several thousand tasks (activities), executed by hundreds of departments or subcontractors. In such cases, it is easier to organize and manage these projects as subprojects of a master project. At times, even though the project is not very big, some tasks may be dependent on several other projects that are external to the project organization. We discuss here about using MS-Project in such cases.

Types of Dependencies

Let us first understand what is meant by dependency as it is one of the most important elements of creating a project schedule network. Previously we discussed about four types of relationships between tasks. The relationship describes how tasks relate to each other (how start and finish of predecessor and successor tasks are related). Dependency determines the order of sequence or activity. It is subtly different from relationships. There are three primary types of dependencies:

1. *Mandatory Dependencies*: These are dependencies that create firm relationships between two activities.

   Example: Testing can start only after the coding is completed.

2. *Discretionary Dependencies*: These types of dependencies enable the project manager to optimize the flow of work throughout the project life cycle and are also known as "soft logic." This works as a tool that the project manager utilizes to create *float* in the schedule. This is a much more effective manner to drive the time line than *hard coding* dates into the schedule (or using constraints in MS-Project).

   Examples: If a team is travelling to a foreign country for say beta testing at a customer location, a discretionary task prior to this task may be to train the team in the language and culture of that region.

3. *External Dependencies*: These are dependencies that are outside the control of the project team. However, these must be reflected in the project schedule.

   Example: A software development project may depend on the procurement of the hardware. Here the procurement of the hardware is outside the control of the project team and is outside the scope of the project.

Tasks or phases in one project, being dependent on the tasks in other (one or more) project is also a case of external dependency. There may be other reasons for dependencies between projects. If a task in a project uses resources that have been assigned to tasks of another project, then also you may have to delay the start of the task till the resources complete the first task.

You can show such dependencies by linking tasks between projects in MS-Office Project. External predecessor and successor tasks have grayed task names and Gantt bars. Such tasks are also referred to as Ghost tasks.

Example Problem: Creating an External Dependency

Let us consider a case in which a small project of software testing t has been planned. Let us say this particular project is also dependent on setting up the hardware. In this exercise, you link tasks in these two project plans, and you see the results in the two project plans. Copy **Dependency** subfolder to your working directory from **Practice-Files/Ch09**

1. On the **File** tab, click **Open**. The Open dialog box appears.
2. Navigate to the **Dependency** subfolder in your working directory and double click the **Testing-project.mpp** file. View the tasks in the Gantt Chart (Figure 9.1).

   On the **File** tab, click **Open**. Navigate to the **Dependency** sub-folder in your working directory, and double-click the **hw-setup.mpp** file. The tasks related to procurement and setting up of the hardware are displayed in the Gantt Chart as shown in Figure 9.2. Note that both the project files are open now.
3. In *hw-setup* in the **Task Name** column, click on task 3 *Install OS & setup the network*.

   You need to finish the task Install OS & setup the network before you begin the task Setup Environment for Testing in the Testing plan; so you will create a dependency between the two plans.
4. On the **View** tab, in the **Window** group, click **Switch Windows**, and then select *Testing-project*. On the **View** tab, in the **Task Views** group, click **Gantt Chart**. The Gantt Chart view appears. Click the name of task 6, *Setup Environment for Testing*. On the **Task** tab, in the **Editing** group, click **Scroll to Task**. Project scrolls the Gantt

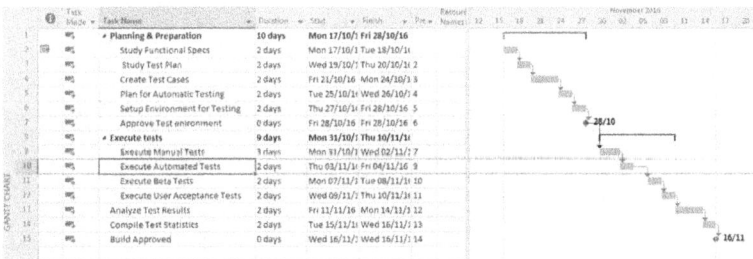

Figure 9.1 Gantt chart for testing

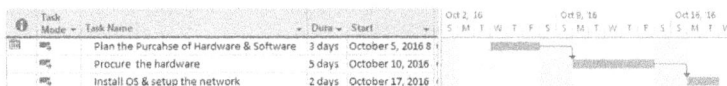

Figure 9.2 Gantt chart for hardware setup (hw-setup project)

Chart view to display task number six. The Predecessor column may not be visible. In the Gantt Chart view, drag the vertical divider bar of the entry table, to the right until the Predecessor column is visible. In the Predecessor field for task 6, click in the field so that the cursor appears directly after the existing predecessor, value 5.

An external predecessor link is created by entering the task in the following format: File Name\Task ID. Directly after the existing predecessor value 5, type hw-setup\3 (with no space between 5 and the comma and the subsequent text). Here hw-setup is located in the same directory. However, in case if the file is located in some other directory, you may have to specify the entire path (or command).

5. Press **Enter**.

MS-Project inserts the external predecessor task named *Install OS & setup the network* into the project (in addition to existing predecessor Plan for Automatic Testing). The external task represents task 3 from the hw-setup project. The external task's Gantt bar and the task name appear in gray as shown in Figure 9.3. If you point to the external task's Gantt bar, MS-Project displays a Screen tip that contains information about the external task, including the full path of the external project plan in which the ghost task resides.

6. Optionally, you can also look at the ghost task in the project plan as the plan window is open. On the **View** tab, in the **Window** group, click **Switch Windows**, click *hw-setup* in the **Task Name** column, and select the name of task, *Install OS & setup the network*. Adjust the chart portion of the Gantt Chart view to display the selected tasks. To do that on the **View** tab, in the **Zoom** group, click **Selected Tasks**.

You can see that task 3, Install OS & setup the network, is a predecessor for the external task Setup Environment for Testing.

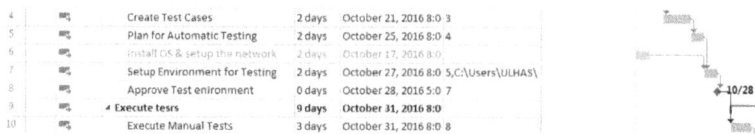

4		Create Test Cases	2 days	October 21, 2016 8:0	3	
5		Plan for Automatic Testing	2 days	October 25, 2016 8:0	4	
6		Install OS & setup the network	2 days	October 17, 2016 8:0		
7		Setup Environment for Testing	2 days	October 27, 2016 8:0	5,C:\Users\ULHAS\	
8		Approve Test enironment	0 days	October 28, 2016 5:0	7	10/28
9		⊿ Execute tesrs	9 days	October 31, 2016 8:0		
10		Execute Manual Tests	3 days	October 31, 2016 8:0	8	

Figure 9.3 External predecessor is Install OS & setup the network is inserted in Testing project (displayed in Gray)

However, it has no effect on other tasks here as Setup Environment for Testing is a successor task with no other links to this project.

You have the option of breaking the link between these plans. There is bidirectional associativity. That means, deleting a task in the source plan or the ghost task in the destination plan deletes the corresponding task or ghost task in the other plan.

7. Save all open files and Close the session.

Note: You may turn off the display of cross-project links using Project Options for the file. To do this, on the **File** tab, click **Options**. In the **Project Options** dialog box, on the **Advanced** tab, clear the **Show External Successors** and **Show External Predecessors** check-boxes.

Master Project and Subprojects

Before discussing how we can track multiple schedules by grouping together into a master in MS-Office Project, let us discuss about subprojects and the benefits of creating smaller projects in a software like MS-Project. Subprojects are usually areas of project that are either outsourced to a different department or to vendors. The vendor or the department may have specialized knowledge or technology. For example, if you are a contractor specialized in software product development, you may have outsourced the development of user interface design to a firm that specializes in the same.

In MS-Project, we can think of a master project as a collection of consolidated projects that show hierarchy among multiple related projects. In the master project, subprojects appear as summary tasks, which you can expand. (Please also see Figure 9.4 to understand the benefits of using subprojects.)

In MS-Project, we may be using subprojects for one or more of the following reasons:

1. It is easier to independently plan, schedule, and control multiple projects (subprojects) than planning, scheduling, and controlling a single mega-project.
2. It is helpful in overall corporate reporting and planning. It makes decision making easier in the company.

3. You may be working on multiple projects, with same set of resources, simultaneously. Managing resource assignments is easier in such cases.

4. The project is executed in different sites or departments. Your organization is not centralized. In a decentralized or distributed environment, a master project and subprojects give workers more control over their own work than one centralized project file does.

There are various ways of consolidating subprojects into a master project. Let us first try out the same without using a resource pool. For this, you require three files stored in the subfolder Files-for-consolidation.

Benefits of using a master project

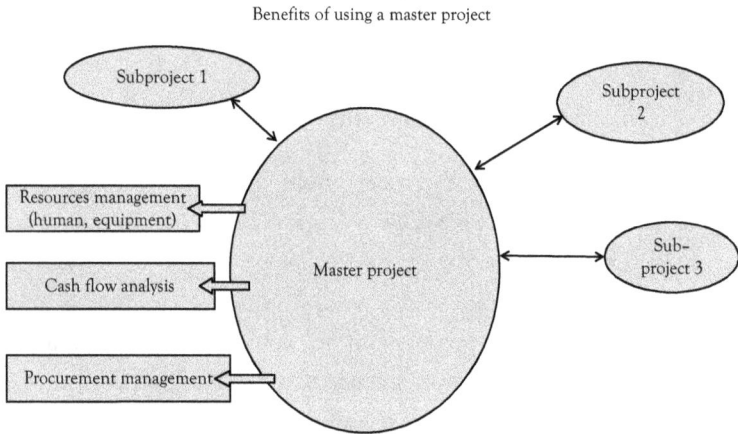

Figure 9.4 *Benefits of using master project and subprojects*

Example Problem: Consolidating Multiple Projects

Let us consider a case in which there are two small software projects to be consolidated. For that, copy the folder **Files-for-consolidation** from **Practice-files/Ch09** to your working directory. There are two subprojects namely *AppDevelopment* and *Testing-project*. Let us say these are managed by a single contractor (or company). These will utilize some common resources.

To get a hang of activities and resources associated with each of these subprojects you may have a look at Gantt Chart and Resource—Sheets of each of these. Double click and open all two files. Observe the Gantt Chart and Resource Sheet views of the files for each of these projects (Figures 9.5–9.8). You will notice that some resources are common between projects.

Let us try consolidating these two files in to one master file using some options available in MS-Project. (Note: The users who are not in US, may receive an error message stating that "The files you are consolidating are of different currencies. ...." during the consolidation process. That is because the new master file you would create might have a different currency by default. That will not block the process of consolidation though. However, you may change the currency of the master project file as explained in Chapter 5.)

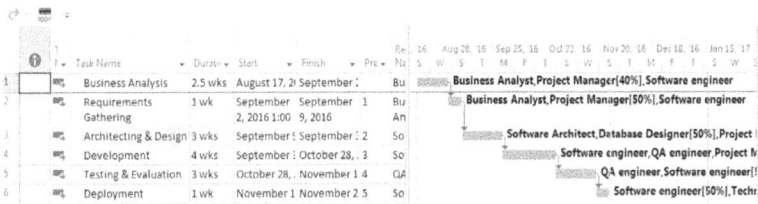

Figure 9.5 Gantt chart for AppDevelopment project

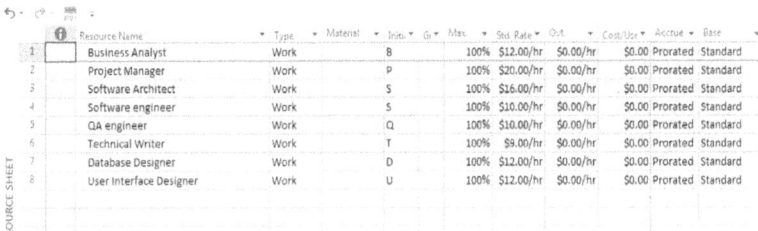

Figure 9.6 Resource sheet forAppDevelopment

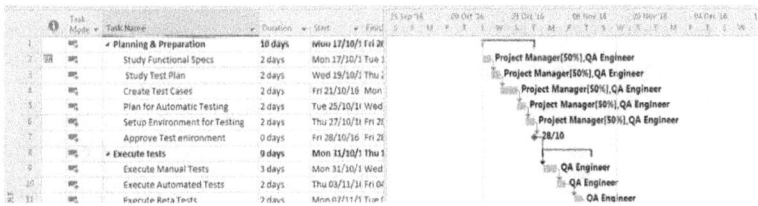

Figure 9.7 Gantt chart for testing project

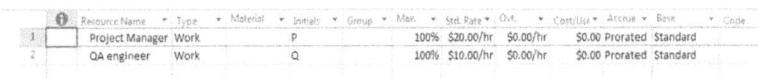

Figure 9.8 Resource sheet for testing project

Using Copy/Paste for Creating a Master Project

An easier way to produce a master project is **Copy/Paste.** Here we create an empty master project to start with and populate it with copy/paste. (As mentioned earlier, copy the folder Files-for-consolidation from **Practice-files/Ch09** to your working directory and rename it suitably.)

1. Open a **New** file and save it as a **Master.mpp** in the same folder as the other two project files. Select **Options** from the **File** tab. Options dialog appears. In the **Advanced** options, select **Show project summary task** check-box, under **Display Options for This Project.**

   (Note: (a) The same can also be done clicking on the **Format** tab, then selecting **Summary Task** and **Project Summary Task** check-boxes under the **Show/Hide** group. (b) This process of showing project summary task may have to be repeated for other subprojects too.)

   By default the Project start date is current date and you may set it suitably. Now open **AppDevelopment** project. Click the **expand/collapse** arrow next to AppDevelopment's project summary task to collapse the detail. This is a *very important* step. Click the **ID 0** to highlight the whole summary and the whole project. Right click to get the contextual or pull-down menu and select **Copy** from there as shown in Figure 9.9. (Note: The same may be achieved using Copy and Paste buttons of the **Clipboard** group under the **Task** tab)

2. Go to the master and select the next blank task. Click the **Paste** button. **AppDevelopment** should now appear in **Master.** Click the **expand/collapse** arrow next to AppDevelopment's project summary task to collapse the detail. This is a very *important* step.

3. Now click the next task cell. Here we have to copy **Testing project** using the same process. If you do not collapse the detail of AppDevelopment, when you paste Testing project, it will be indented under the last task of AppDevelopment. Also, you need not have to scroll down to find the last task if you collapse the subproject.

We created a master project as shown in Figure 9.10. However, you notice that all the subprojects start at the same project start date. You

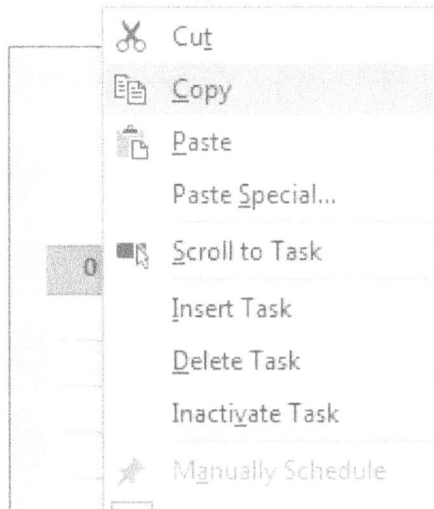

Figure 9.9 Copy the AppDevelopment project with shortcut menu

Figure 9.10 Master project created using Copy/Paste

also find that the master project and subprojects are not associated in a dynamic way, which means that the changes made to the master project will not be reflected in the individual subprojects and vice versa. Close all open files using the **File** tab.

Using Insert Project Without a Resource Pool

In the second method, we shall use the Insert Project feature to consolidate. Initially, we use this as it is and analyze the result. Subsequently, we shall improve upon the same using an additional file known as *resource pool*. Here are the steps required:

1. Copy the folder **Files-for-consolidation** to your working directory again say as **Files-for-consolidation-no-pool**. Create a new master project. Select **New** from the **File** tab. Select the template **Blank**

Project from the template list. This will create a new blank project. Save this as a **Master-without-pool** in the same folder as subprojects.

2. Click in the first Task Name cell of the Master Project Gant Chart. From the **Project** tab, select **Subproject** in the **Insert** group (Figure 9.11). **A File Selection** dialog will pop up. From your appropriate directory, select *AppDevelopment* and click the **Insert** button at the bottom (Figure 9.12), or double click the project name. When you insert projects, to make sure the results are dynamic, we need to link them with the master. So when you select to insert *AppDevelopment*, make sure the **link to** the **project** box is checked. In the master project, subprojects appear as summary tasks that you can easily arrange in an outline.

3. Make sure AppDevelopment is collapsed (click on the expand/collapse arrow next to the task name if required). Now repeat the process for *Testing-project* subproject. When these get inserted, then expand all by clicking on both expand/collapse arrows as shown in Figure 9.13, and have a look at the Resource Sheet view. You will see that the resources have been repeated for all these and numbered separately, as shown in Figure 9.14. Let us understand why this happens.

When we used this method (inserting subprojects without resource pool) of consolidation, MS-Project consolidated resources and tasks from subprojects into one file. While doing so, the resources were aggregated as it is (Figure 9.15) and hence we find duplicate entries for resources like *Project*

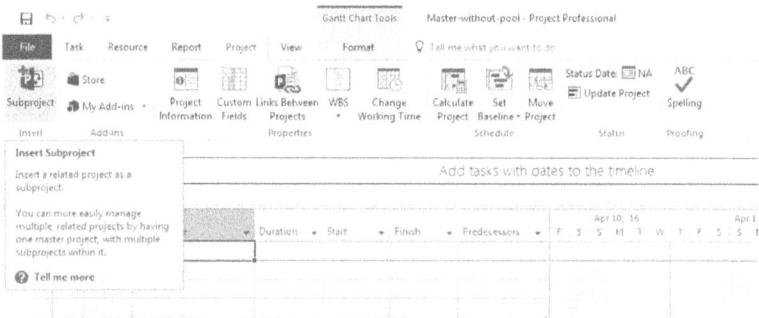

Figure 9.11 Using insert subproject option to create master project

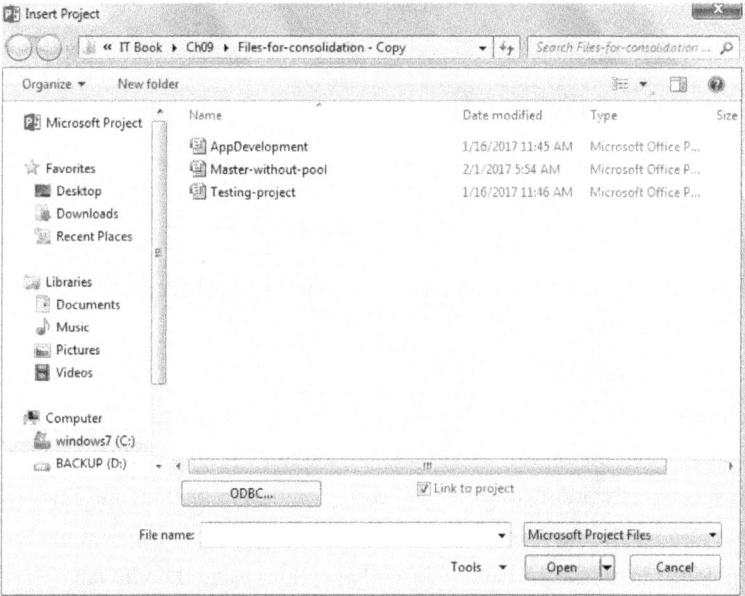

Figure 9.12 *Navigate and select subproject for insertion*

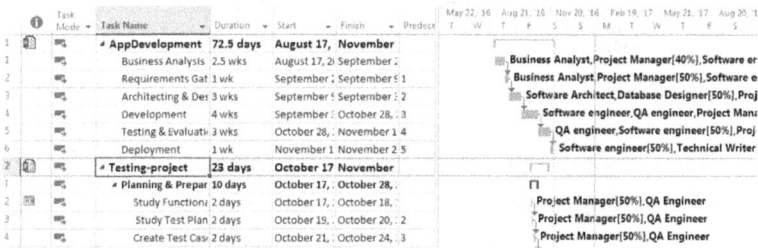

Figure 9.13 *Gantt Chart of the master project created with Insert subproject*

Figure 9.14 *Resource Sheet of the master project, without pool (observe the duplicate resources)*

Master Project

Project 1	Project 2	Project 3
• Resource details 1	• Resource details 2	• Resource details 3

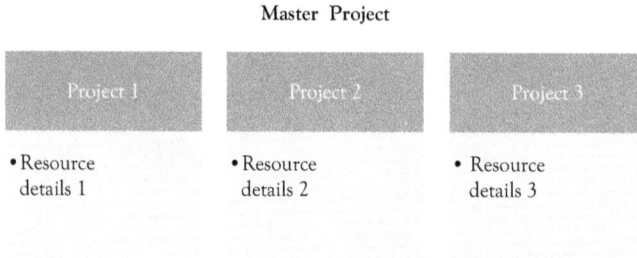

Figure 9.15 Master project without a resource pool (conceptual representation)

Manager and Labor in the Resource Sheet of the master file. The resource names should not repeat (For example, though there are two different Project Managers working on these projects, there has to be only one entry for that resource in the resource sheet of the master project). The next method will take care of the problem. Close all open files using the **File** tab.

Using a Resource Pool for Consolidation

The earlier method of inserting subprojects had the problem of duplication of resources. The problem of duplicate resources appearing in the Resource Sheet of consolidated projects can be solved by using a resource pool. Let us first understand what it is. The project manager has a team of resources available (like analyst, coder, tester) but she or he does not know how many will be required, and whether she or he can even do the multiple projects with the resources available. We therefore need to set up a resource pool and associate each project with that pool, as shown in Figure 9.16. With a resource pool, all the resource information that resides in the pool appears in each project file that shares the pool, because the resource pool will be linked to the projects. The resource pool is nothing but a project file with only resources and no tasks.

Now we shall do the consolidation exercise with a resource pool. Again you require subproject files.

1. Copy the folder **Files-for-consolidation** (containing files) from **Practice-files/Ch09** to your working directory, say as **Files-for-consolidation-pool**

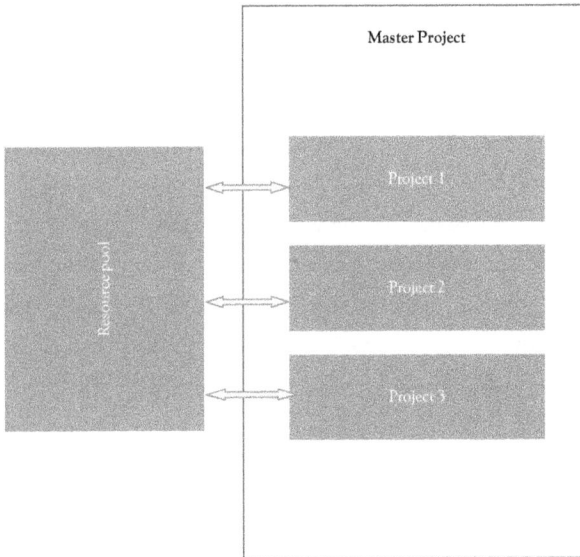

Figure 9.16 Master project with a shared resource pool (conceptual representation)

2. Create a new empty project file and select **New** from the **File** tab. Select **Blank Project**.

Save the file in the same folder with a representative name. Select **Save As** from the **File** tab. Navigate to the folder containing subprojects, that is, **Files-for-consolidation-pool** and save the file as **Resources-pool.**

Select **Resource Sheet** from **Resource Views** group of **View** Tab. This file is an empty project file and as of now does not contain any tasks and resources.

Since this file does not contain resources, it has to be populated with all the available resources. This can be done by opening each of the subproject file and sharing resources with the pool file. For this, we open all the subproject files by double clicking on each of those files. (You may also arrange all project plans within the MS-Project window. To do that, on the **View** tab, in the **Window** group, click **Arrange All**. This step is not a must; however, this will enable you to view changes in the Resource Sheet, as and when they occur.)

3. You will see the Resource Sheet of the common pool file **Resources-pool.**

Click on the title bar of the **AppDevelopment** project plan. On the **Resource** tab, in the **Assignments** group, click on **Resource Pool**, and then select **Share Resources** as shown in Figure 9.17.

The Share Resources dialog box appears. Under Resources for *AppDevelopment* select the **Use resources** option, as shown in Figure 9.18. Any open project plan can be used as a resourcepool and the *Use Resources From* list contains all such project plans. (Note: In case the pull-down list is not active, toggle with Radio Buttons and come back). Select *Resources-pool.* Click **OK** to close the Share Resources dialog box. Under **On conflict with calendar or resource information**, make sure that the **Pool takes precedence** option is selected.

You will see that the resource information from the *AppDevelopment* project would appear in the Resources-pool file as shown in

Figure 9.17 Click Share Resources in the Assignments group, to start linking with a resource pool

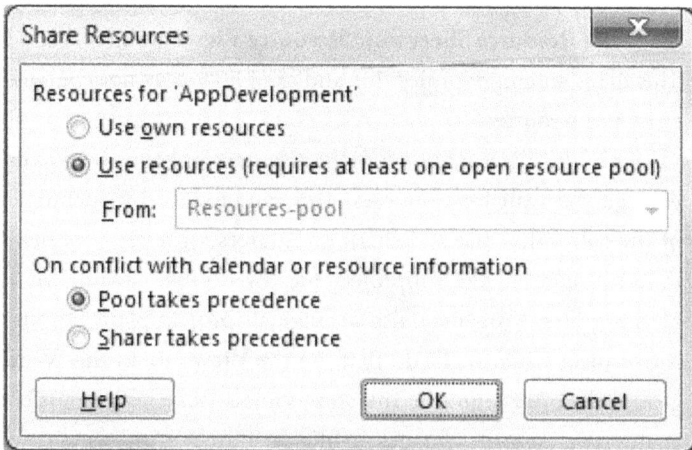

Figure 9.18 Share resources dialog

Figure 9.19. (Click on the *Resource-pool* file window and switch to *Resource Sheet* view to verify.)

4. Similarly, you would have to set up **Testing-project** plans as a sharer plan with the same resource pool. With this, you are ready with a common resource pool file, which contains all resources of the three subprojects (without any duplication of resource names). This can be verified by going through the Resource Sheet of common pool file Resources pool.

5. Now create a blank master file and insert three subprojects as discussed in the earlier case (when you select to insert subproject, make sure the link box is checked).

With this, we complete the third method of consolidating (Figure 9.20). The results are dynamic (with a kind of bidirectional associativity), in that any change to the master project will be reflected in the individual projects and vice versa. You can delete the master if you

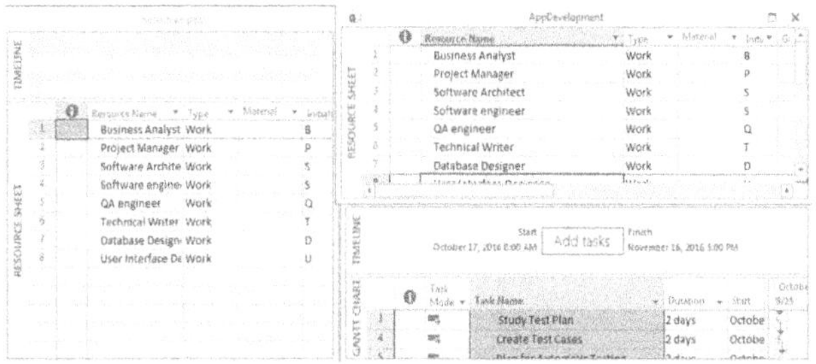

Figure 9.19 Resource sheet of the pool file gets populated as you share resources

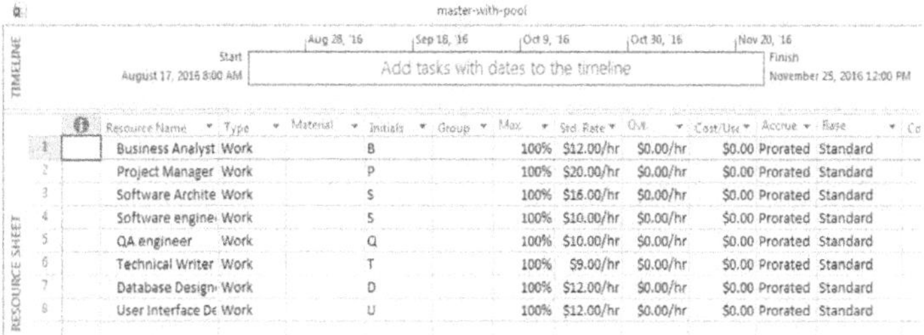

Figure 9.20 Resource sheet of master project (created with a resource pool)

want to and the individual projects will retain the changes when you save them. Later you can always recreate the master, or another master with a different set of projects. Close all open files using the **File** tab,

To conclude, in this chapter, we did study various methods of consolidating projects in this project and also how a resource pool can aid the process. We also did discuss about creating an external dependency in a project in this chapter. MS-Project Professional, although not exclusively meant for managing multiple projects, allows you to create resource pools and thereby administer resources in a centralized fashion to a sufficient degree.

CHAPTER 10

Beyond Scope, Time, and Cost

Objectives

On completion of this chapter, you should be able to

1. Understand the use of MS-Project in different knowledge areas with examples

In previous chapters, we discussed about using MS-Project for managing scope, schedule, and cost of a project. However, MS-Project can very well be used to manage other project constraints like quality and risks. The purpose of this chapter is to provide you methods of using MS-Project to manage processes related to other knowledge areas. Not all the project management processes are simply transposed to MS-Project and some may not be managed in MS-Project at all. This chapter provides you techniques to manage your projects with MS-Project and the *Project Management Body of Knowledge* (*PMBOK*®) *Guide* processes. Table 10.1 gives some examples of using MS-Project in managing project management processes from other knowledge areas like quality.

As discussed earlier, Table 10.1 is representative only and MS-Project can be used in many different ways as a tool or as a means to generate inputs for various processes. The following examples explain in detail how one can use some features of MS-Project for managing project management processes.

Example Problem: Planning Quality Management Using MS-Project

As we discussed earlier we can use MS-Project for quality management processes too. This particular example deals with quality standards of a

Table 10.1 Some sample processes in which MS-Project can be used

PMBOK® process	How MS-Project can be used
Plan quality management	Relevant standards and regulations for each task can be recorded in the Task Notes or a user-definable field. Hyper Text Mark-up Language (HTML) link can also be used to refer to a relevant standard of the task.
Manage Quality	MS-Project also allows you to create project templates and use them subsequently. For quality audits, such templates can be created and used. These help as tools in the Manage Quality Assurance process.
Control quality	1. You can analyze variances and trends using visual reports. This can help you in quality control. 2. Additional activities (tasks) should be included in the schedule for checking Quality.
Plan Resources management	1. All people involved in a project may be entered into the Resource Sheet. Information about resources may be entered into either existing fields or user-definable fields (as MS-Project allows you to define your own custom field). This may include roles, responsibilities, and the project organizational structure. 2. Resources may be grouped using the Grouping function and an organizational structure may be created in a table format.
Manage communications	Once the reporting requirements get defined then the MS-Project Tables and Reports may be used effectively to create reports for various project stakeholders.
Identify risks	1. Analyzing a Gantt Chart schedule of a project can help you identify risks related to resources and so on. 2. User-defined field feature may be used to assign a risk log item number and description in the Entry table or in the Resource Sheet.
Monitor risks	If you are familiar with Visual Basic® for Applications, you can use it to create macros in MS-Project to alert you when trigger events occur. This can help you to identify new risks and then respond to them appropriately.

mobile app development project. The Android coding style, which is available on the Internet, has to be associated with the Development task in the project. The guided example explains the steps involved in using a hyperlink to associate quality standards.

1. Double click and open the project file. (Copy Sample Project file **AppDevelopment-start.mpp** from the **Practice-Files/Ch10** folder and save as **AppDevelopment.mpp**) The file will open with a task list as shown in Figure 10.1. Click on the **View** tab and select **Gantt.**

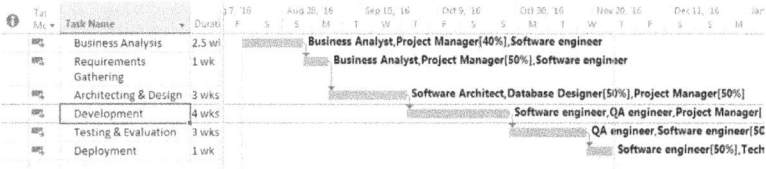

Figure 10.1 Open project file AppDevelopment-start, to insert a hyperlink

Let us say you want to associate the standard with the task *Development*. A hyperlink can be inserted by right clicking the task and selecting **Link** from the contextual menu that appears as shown in Figure 10.2.

2. You get **Insert Hyperlink** dialog box as shown in Figure 10.3. There is a "Text to display" box. Here, you have to type the text you want to appear with the hyperlink indicator. (Note: Indicators are small icons representing information for a task or resource that is displayed in the Indicators field. The Indicators field is located to the right of the ID field and appears in a number of tables.) As you see later, when you move the cursor to the Indicators field, the text appears explaining the hyperlink. Enter the text *Android Coding Style*.

3. Although you have added a name to the link, you have yet to specify the website. Click the **Browse the Web** button (icon with a lens, in the middle) to start your Web browser, and then copy the web address (*https://source.android.com/source/code-style* in this case) from the Address box of the browser and paste it into the Address box in

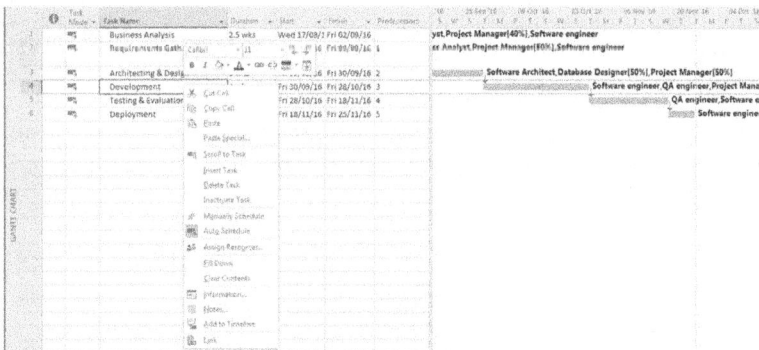

Figure 10.2 Select link from shortcut menu of the task

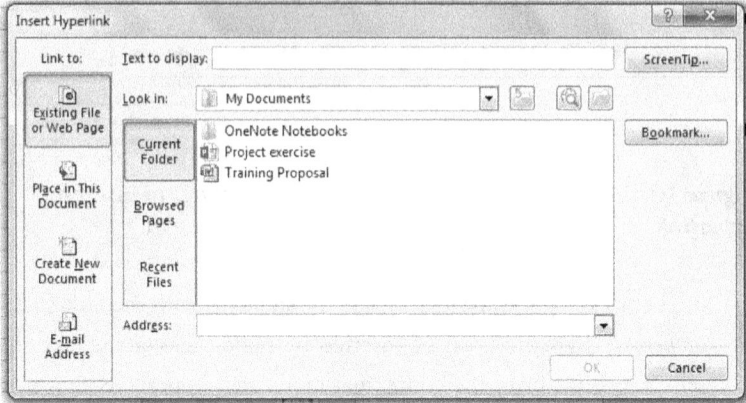

Figure 10.3 Insert hyperlink dialog box

the **Insert Hyperlink** dialog box. Press **OK** and this will complete the process of creating the Hyperlink.

4. Now you can observe the Hyperlink icon in the Indicator column of the task Development. You can also verify whether the link is working. For that, move the cursor in the Indicator column of the task *Development.* A screen tip displays the link description *Android coding style* as shown in Figure 10.4. The cursor changes in shape (fist with finger pointing up), pointing to the existence of an HTML link. When you click the link, a separate browser window pops up to navigate you to the website of Android coding style.

Close the file.

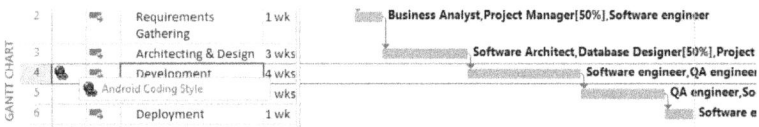

Figure 10.4 Link descriptions get displayed by a screen tip, when you move the cursor over the hyperlink indicator

Example Problem: Using MS-Project for Creating Risk Register

A risk register is created during risk identification by the project team and contains information on project risks. This document gets updated with other risk management processes (perform qualitative analysis of risks, control risks, etc.). In a project, to start with, a risk register contains information on identified risks and their root causes. Subsequently, as the project progresses, risk analysis is carried out on a regular basis and the register is updated with information like ranking, probability, impact, and status (like retired). In MS-Project, you can attach notes to tasks and resources. This feature can be effectively utilized to create a Risk Register. As we progress with the project, this document can be updated to include information like new risks, risk mitigation plan, and contingency plans.

With the help of an example we shall understand how attaching notes to tasks helps you to build a risk register. The guided example deals with linking a risk register created in Microsoft Excel to a small project for Software enhancement.

1. For this, you need the file **enhancement-start.mpp** and **Risk Register-Software-Project.xls** in your working directory. Copy these files from the **Practice-files/Ch10** folder. Rename **the enhancement-start.mpp** as **enhancement.mpp** and open the project plan by double clicking on **enhancement.mpp** file (Figure 10.5). In the **View** tab, **Zoom** group, select **Zoom Entire Project** and view the entire project.

2. Check whether Project Summary Task is displayed. It should be. If it is not displayed (for any reason), select **File** and then **Options.** The **Project options** dialog pops up.

   Select **Advanced** and click on the check-box **Show Project Summary Task** (under **Display Options for This Project**).

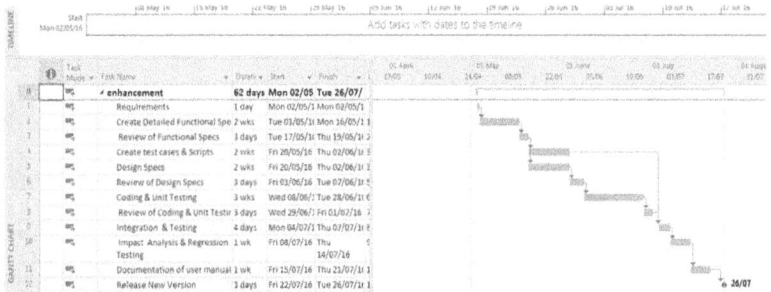

Figure 10.5 Chart of the enhancement project

3. Select the top-level summary task, that is, *enhancement*. In the **Task** tab, **Properties** group, click on **Task Notes**. The **Task Information** dialog box will pop up with the **Notes** tab highlighted as shown in Figure 10.6. (Another way of doing the same is to double click on the task, and then select the **Notes** tab in the **Task Information** dialog that pops up.)

4. You can enter plain text in the dialog to create simple notes (known as *Short Notes*) or you can embed a file like drawing or spreadsheet (to create *Long Notes*). The objective here is to embed a spreadsheet. Click on the **Insert Object** button (button with arrow) on the **Summary Task Information** dialog box. The **Insert Object** dialog box will appear. Select the **Create from File** radio button (Figure 10.7).

5. Click on the **Browse** button and select the file **RiskRegister-Software-Project.xls** from your working folder. This worksheet contains information on risks such as probability, impact, and cause of the risk event and gets embedded as notes for this specific task. (Note: In the Excel spreadsheet, only qualitative values of probability and impact of risks are indicated)

6. The next step is to confirm that the notes are attached. Once you attach notes, you will observe that the indicator column of Summary task has a notes graphic attached to it as shown in Figure 10.8. Move the cursor there. If there are short notes (text, without any embedded object), then they get displayed as the screen tip.

7. In this case, long notes are attached and you have to double click on the Notes icon. The **Task Information** dialog then pops up

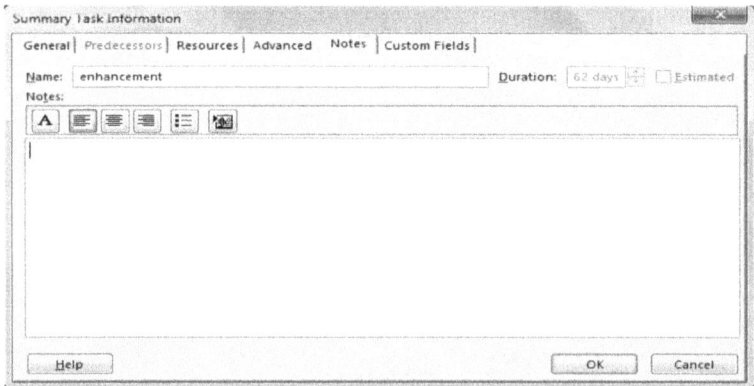

Figure 10.6 Task information dialog box

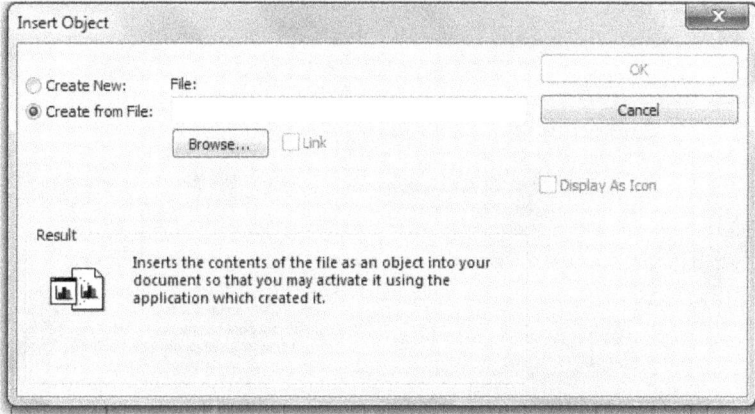

Figure 10.7 *Creating an object and inserting it as task notes*

displaying the notes you added as shown in Figure 10.9. You may double click on the displayed notes, in the dialog, to activate the relevant application (Microsoft Excel in this case). This shall help you to update the risk register during project execution. (Notes can also be used in case of resources to add additional information.)

Close all files.

To conclude, we discussed in this chapter how MS-Project can be used in processes related to different knowledge areas (knowledge areas not related to project time management and project cost management). Although the discussion is about managing a single project, we can extend the same to a consolidated project. Similarly, although we have considered here processes defined in *PMBOK®* we can very well use MS-Project for processes defined through other similar standards or framework.

Figure 10.8 **Notes indicator in MS-Project**

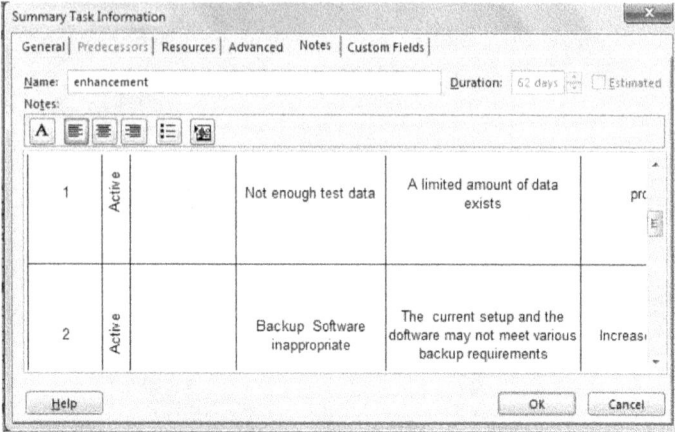

Figure 10.9 Notes are displayed in the dialog and you may double click to start the relevant application

CHAPTER 11

Managing Agile Projects Using MS-Project

Objectives

On completion of the chapter you should be able to

1. Understand the use of Agile Templates in MS-Project
2. Understand about the Sprints and Backlog tasks
3. Understand how custom fields in MS-Project can help Agile Project Management

In previous chapters, we did discuss how we can use Microsoft Project to plan and track Information Technology Projects. However, we did not discuss about using MS-Project for managing Agile Projects. Though there are software tools available in the market to manage projects specifically based on Agile Methodology, we can use some features of MS-Project for the same.

In the recent past, Microsoft has introduced templates for the agile project, which provide agile specific views, fields, and so on. If you are connected to the Internet, you will get a list of templates when you start the MS-Project professional as shown in Figure 11.1 (observe the right-most box on the second row, mentioning Agile Project Management). Note that this chapter was written based on such features available as of August 2017. Microsoft has been adding new templates, columns, and so on, to support Agile Methodologies. If you download the latest version, you may find more features supporting Agile. This chapter may not discuss some of the newly released Agile capabilities.

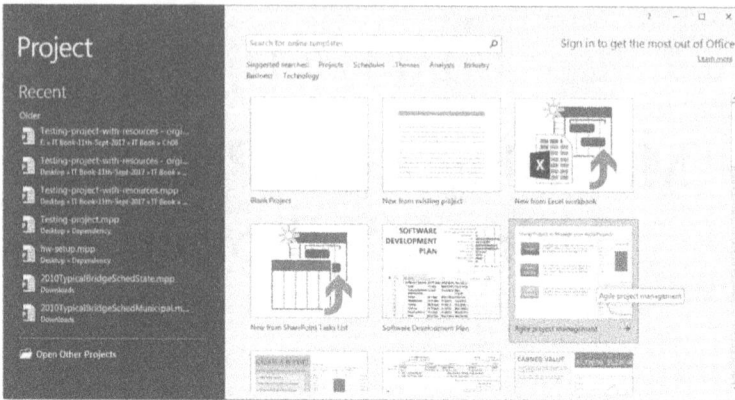

Figure 11 .1 MS-Project offers the option of using agile template if your computer is connected to the Internet.

Once you select the template, you get an interface to specify a date and start with a new Agile project (Figure 11.2). Next, you have the option of selecting an Agile specific view like Sprints view, Product Backlog view as shown in Figure 11.3. Let us say, you select the *Sprints*, you get a template with Sprints view containing corresponding fields like Sprint number as shown in Figure 11.4. You may explore and close the template file.

Understanding Scrum

Before taking up an exercise to see how we can use MS-Project for Agile Project Management, let us take a quick look at Scrum.

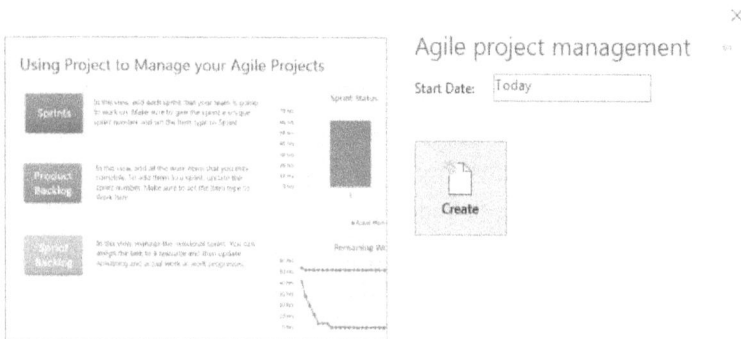

Figure 11.2 Use the template and create a new agile project

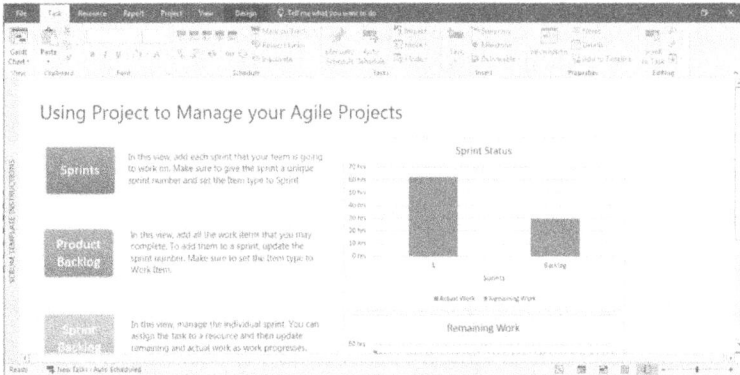

Figure 11.3 Select the agile specific view like sprints view to start with

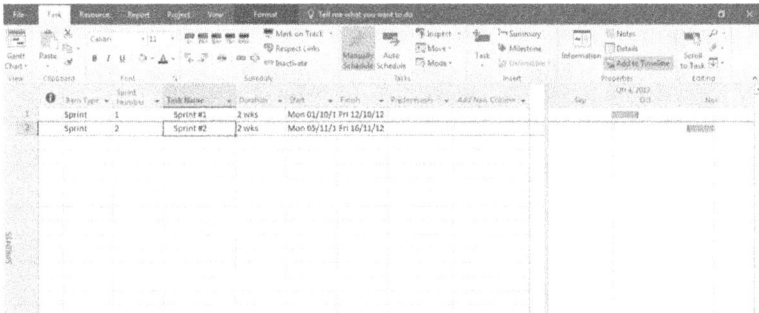

Figure 11.4 An Agile project template with the sprint view

Scrum, the most widely practiced Agile process, has been successfully used in software development. Scrum divides complex work into simple pieces, to be delivered by small teams, so that the far reaching work of a large project is visible in short time horizons called sprints.

Scrum begins with the product vision which gets translated into the product backlog. Product backlog is an important shared tool and contains a list of everything that could be done over the lifetime of the project. The product backlog is divided and defined into items that can be delivered independently of each other.

Once the product backlog has been established, the team can start sprinting. To start a sprint, first step the team has to take up is to conduct sprint planning. Items at the top of the backlog are worked on initially, so they need to be well defined, or ready. The sprint backlog consists of all items that need to be completed by the end of the sprint and reflects the priority order of the product backlog. Once the sprint backlog is finalized, only in rare circumstances changes are done. Figure 11.5 depicts a typical sprint with product backlog and so on.

A couple of other relevant terms which we should know to go ahead are:

- Customer need: Help you prioritize or rank activities in order of importance (like high, low);
- Story points: As doing a full estimation of the work up front may be inefficient, story points mechanism is used for estimating the size of the overall work being requested (and also for measuring whether you have too much complexity in a sprint);
- State: State of the task (like open, closed).

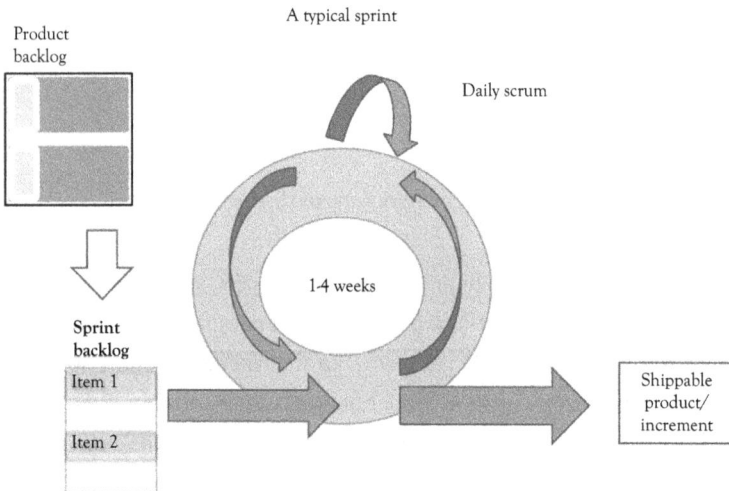

Figure 11.5 A typical Sprint with Product backlog and so on

Creating Custom Fields for Managing Scrum Projects

Custom Fields help a user to define her or his own customized fields for any particular project. This feature can be used in a scrum project to create own fields. We shall be exploring the same in this exercise.

In this exercise we are opening a project with two sprints. We will add some fields like Story points, Customer need, and State to this project

1. Copy the file **Agile-Project-Management-Start** from the **Practice-files/Ch11** folder to your working directory and rename the same as **Agile-Project-Management.** Double click and open the same. Gantt Chart with sprints will be visible as shown in the Figure 11.6.

2. As a first step create State field. To create State field and other custom fields. Go to the **Project Tab** in the Ribbon. Click on the icon for **Custom Fields** (as shown in Figure 11.7).

3. The **Custom Fields** Dialog pops up. Select the **Task** option using the radio button on the top.

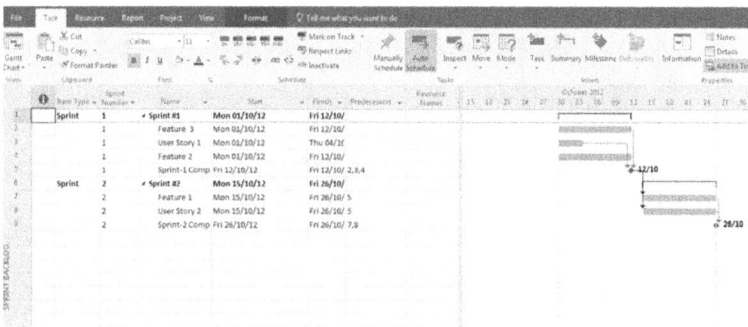

Figure 11.6 The sample file Agile-Project-Management with two sprints (opened in Sprint Backlog View)

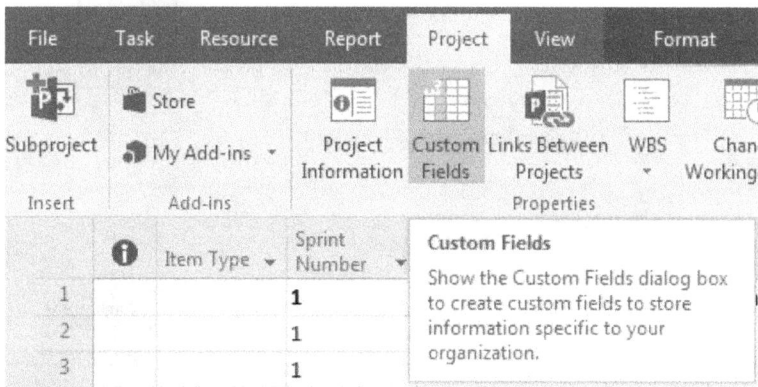

Figure 11.7 Creating a custom field

4. After selecting *Text 3*, Click on the **Rename** button. Rename *Text 3* to *State* as shown in Figure 11.8.

5. Now that you have created a new custom field **State,** next you have to specify possible values for the **State** field. Highlight the **State** field and click on the **Lookup** button. You can fill in the values wanted in the **Lookup table**. In this case fill *Open, Close, In-Progress, Done, Not Done.*

6. To mark a particular choice as the Default value, select the checkbox for **Use a value from the table as a default entry for the field**, in the **Edit Lookup Table for State** dialog as shown in Figure 11.9.

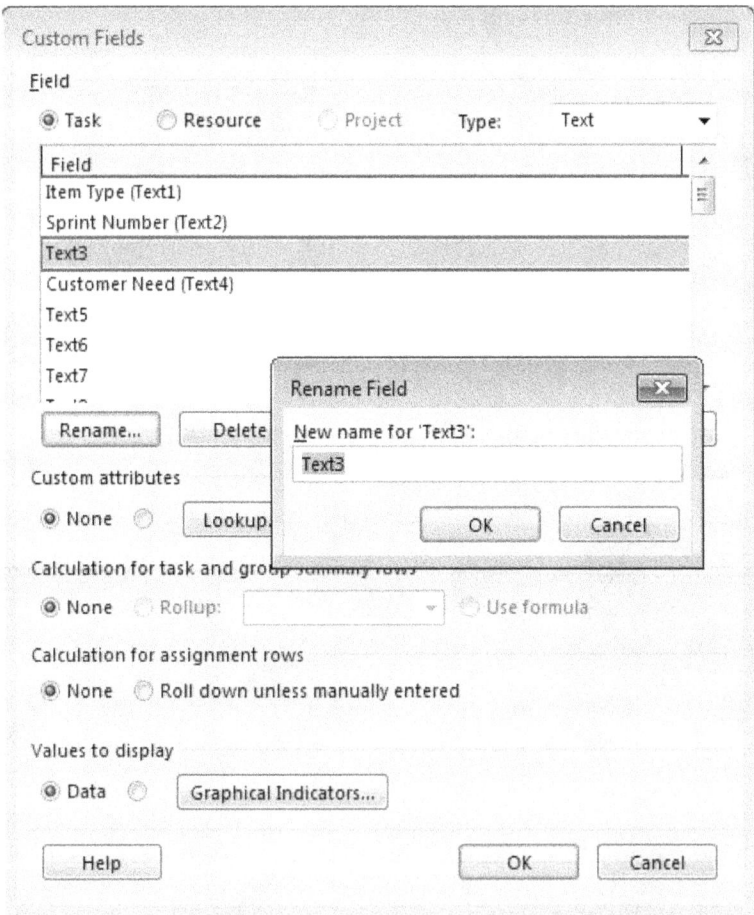

Figure 11.8 Creating a custom field state using rename option

Highlight the choice you want to make the default (in this case *Open*). Click on the **Set Default** button for this value to auto-populate when a task is added to the schedule. Close the **Edit Lookup Table for State dialog.**

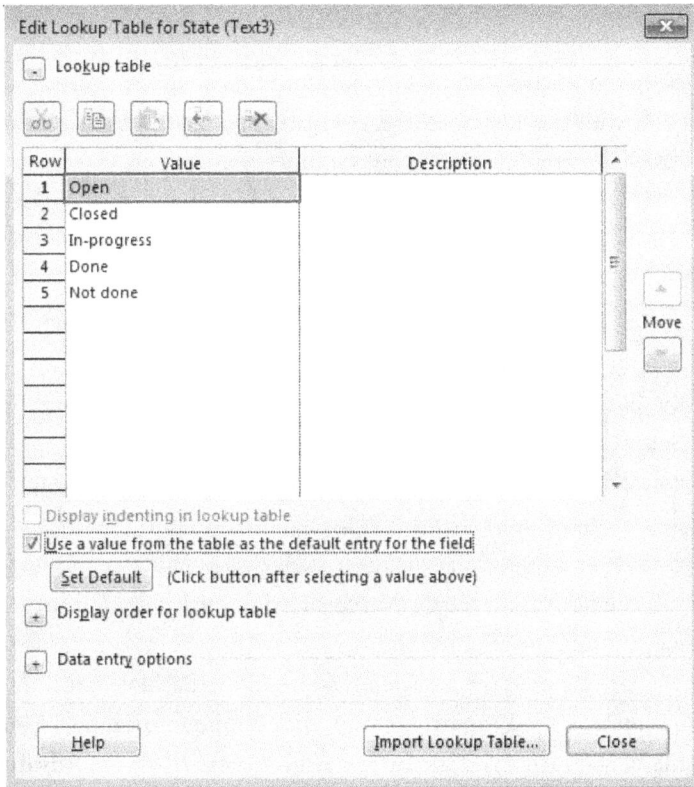

Figure 11.9 Filling in the values for state field and choosing a default value

Notes

1. To test the default setting are working, you may insert a new column with the *State* field and insert a new task in the Gantt Chart. The new task will appear with *Open* value for the State.

2. At times some tasks may not be shown when you apply these changes, because of the filter being applied. Go to the **View** tab, **Data** group and remove the filter using the pull down menu.

We discussed creating a custom field to specify the State of the task. On similar lines you may create custom field like Customer Need, Story Points (a numerical field). You need not close the file as we may continue using the file to discuss some more relevant topics

Backlog Tasks

Earlier we did discuss about the typical sprint. We can also create a summary task with the name Backlog. An agile team will constantly be adding, removing, or reprioritizing tasks in this area.

1. Create a *Backlog* summary task and add 2 subtasks (say *User Story 3* and *User Story 4*) as shown in Figure 11.10 (Please do have a look at Appendix C of the book about creating tasks, etc. if required.) You may also make the Project Summary Task visible. For that click the **Format** Tab and under the **Show/Hide** group select the **Project Summary Task** check-box.

2. For the backlog tasks, we need to make a configuration change. By default, these tasks are set to the default constraint type, *As Soon as Possible*, and we have to change it to *As Late as Possible*. By doing so, you can have the work always scheduled in the future, and then you move it into the required sprint.

    For changing the constraint, select all the Backlog Tasks. In the Task tab, in the **Properties** group, click on the **Information** icon in the Ribbon. In the **Task Information** dialog, select the **Advanced** Tab, and then you can change the constraint type to *As Late as Possible* (Figure 11.11). Close the **Agile-Project-management** file.

Figure 11.10 Add backlog tasks with a summary

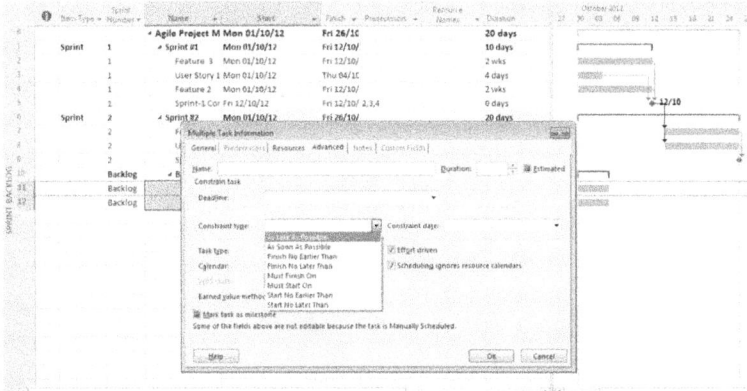

Figure 11.11 Change the constraint type for the backlog tasks

There are many other features of MS-Project which can support agile project management like using burn down charts, setting deadlines for milestones, creating custom groups. We are not discussing the same to keep the discussion short.

To summarize, in this chapter we did look at a typical sprint and how Ms-Project facilitates the agile project planning with templates, custom fields, and so on.

What Is New in MS-Project Professional 2016?

MS-Project Professional has several new features, which include:

1. **Multiple time lines**: You can use multiple time lines feature to highlight different phases of the project or categories of the work. You also have the flexibility of specifying the start and end dates of each of the time line.

2. **Tell me what you want to do**: If you are stuck somewhere and do not know how to go ahead with doing something, enter the related words or phrases. Then you will be able to quickly get to features you want to use or actions you want to perform.

3. **New themes for project**: You now have three office themes to apply to Project 2016: Colorful, Dark Gray, and White. To access these themes, first click **File >Options >General** to see all general options and then click the drop-down menu next to **Office Theme** to select the required theme.

4. **Better control over resources**: In an enterprise environment, some resources may have their time scheduled by a resource manager because of limited availability. With MS-Project Professional 2016 and Project Online, project managers and resource managers can negotiate an agreement, called a **resource engagement**, to make sure that resources are being used appropriately and effectively in the organization.

APPENDIX B

Selecting the Right Edition

Project management solutions of Microsoft can be broadly categorized in to two groups.

- Cloud-based solutions
- On-premises solutions

Project Online Essentials, Project Online Professional, and so on, are part of Cloud-based solutions.

Among On-premises solutions, MS-Project for the desktop is available in two editions:

- *Project Standard*: It is the entry-level application, for individual users, though you can manage multiple projects using the same. You can share documents over the cloud or a network drive.
- *Project Professional*: In addition to features of Project Standard, it has features like Team Planner view and Share-point task list synchronization. You can synchronize information with Project Online. You can also connect to Project server and collaborate, with MS-Project Professional. Project Server architecture has been described in Appendix F.

The book covers Project Standard and Project Professional, though all of the screen shots are of Project Professional. It does not cover the enterprise features available in MS-Project Professional and Project Server.

A Quick Introduction to MS-Project 2016

Introduction

Managing projects effectively is a challenge many managers face. MS-Project 2016 is a software that is designed to assist managers to more effectively manage their projects. It helps them by allowing them to simplify things such as linking tasks, defining work resources, assigning tasks to engineers, visualizing a project, analyzing a project progress, managing a budget, and generating reports. This appendix covers the essentials of MS-Project 2016, provides a brief overview of the graphical user interface, and covers creating and linking tasks, adding resources and assigning them to tasks, and scheduling. This section uses tasks and resources related to a small testing project of Information technology to build an example.

Understanding the User Interface

Microsoft Office Project 2016 incorporates the Ribbon (User interface based on the Fluent), Quick Access toolbar, Back-stage view. Menus and toolbars are context-sensitive. This makes working with MS-Project 2016 easier, for many of you, who are familiar with other MS-Office applications.

The *Gantt Chart* view is the default view and it has two main areas: the task table (left side of the view) and the timescale (right side of the view) as shown in Figure C.1. The *tasktable* lists the project tasks and their accompanying information like start date, duration. The *timescale* displays task bars that correspond to the tasks entered (or listed) in the tasktable. The task bars show the duration of each task, from their planned start dates to their planned finish dates, over time. You can move the separator

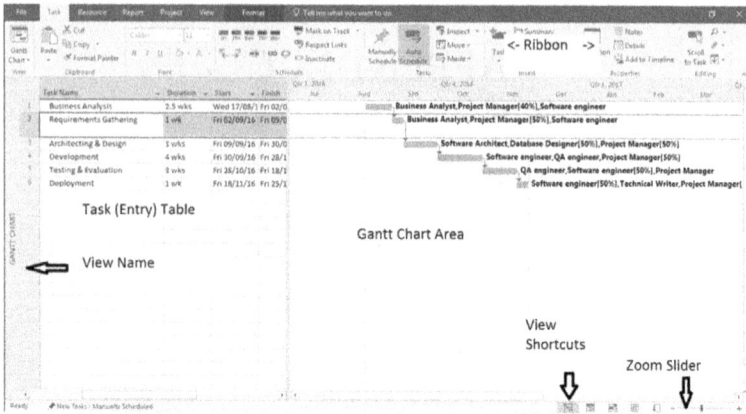

Figure C.1 MS-Project 2016 window with GanttChart view

bar between the timescale and the tasktable to the left or right to display more of either area. The *time line,* which is at the top (included optionally), provides a graphical view of a project along a single left-right axis.

Creating a New Project

To create a new project, you can start with the default blank project, or you can base your new project on an existing project or template. You also have the option of using task lists from other applications like MS-Excel. Let us create a new project from scratch. To create a new project:

1. Click the **Start** button, click **All Programs**, and click **Project 2016**. The **Start** screen appears (see Figure C.2).
2. In the right pane, click **Blank Project** a new, blank project opens in the program window in the **Gantt Chart** view. (You may also do the same by using the **File** tab on the ribbon and then selecting **New** if you are running MS-Project already.)

    Most projects begin with a list of the tasks that need to be completed. Obviously, all the tasks cannot be started on the project start date. Once you create your task list, you have to define the relationships between the tasks.

    Tasks can be manually scheduled or automatically scheduled, depending on the needs of the project and the information currently

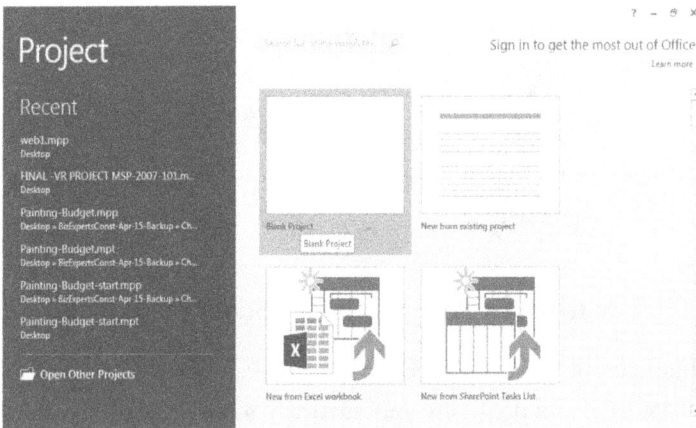

Figure C.2 Creating a new project

available. Generally, when you initiate the project, the information available is limited and you may have to do a macrolevel planning without exact duration and specific start or finish dates. Perhaps, manual scheduling becomes handy at that point of time. At any point during a project, you can change a task to automatic scheduling from manual scheduling, or vice versa.

Creating a Manually Scheduled Task

By default, all new tasks in MS-Project 2016 are set for manual scheduling. With manual scheduling, you can fully control the task's duration, start date, and finish date. The duration can be entered in months (mo), weeks (w), days (d), hours (h), or even in minutes (m). Manually scheduled tasks are marked with the push pin icon, in the Task Mode field.

To create a manually scheduled task:

1. In the first row of the task table, enter *Planning & Preparation* in the **Task Name** Field (see Figure C.3).
2. Enter **10d** in the **Duration** field. This sets the duration of the task to two weeks, as there are five work days in a week.
3. Enter **October 17th, 2016** using the calendar pick in the **Start** field. MS-Project 2016 automatically calculates the finish date using the given information and fills in the **Finish** field. Also, a task bar

Figure C.3 Creating a manually scheduled task

appears in the timescale (on the same row as the task) showing the task's time frame.

Creating an Automatically Scheduled Task

In automatically scheduled task mode, you can have MS-Project 2016 calculate dates and durations. Automatically scheduled tasks are marked with the Gantt-bar icon in the Task Mode field.

Let us create an auto-scheduled task in this plan. To create an automatically scheduled task:

1. In the second row of the task table, in the task name column, enter *Execute Manual Tests* as shown in Figure C.4.
2. Click in the **Task Mode** field, click the down arrow that appears, and then click **Auto Scheduled**. By default, Project2016 assigns the task an estimated duration of one day and automatically fills in the **Duration, Start**, and **Finish** fields. By default, the estimated duration is 1 day (with "?" indicating that you need to key in the data). Also, a task bar appears in the timescale showing the task's time frame.
3. To change the duration of the task to two days, enter **2d** in the **Duration** field. Project 2016 recalculates the finish date and the **Finish** field gets updated accordingly.
4. Similarly add five more Auto-scheduled tasks and respective durations shown in the Table C.1 (in the same order below the second task).

Table C.1 Tasks list (with durations)

Task number	Task name	Duration (days)
3	Execute Automated Tests	2
4	Execute Beta Tests	2
5	Execute User Acceptance Tests	2
6	Analyze Test Results	2
7	Compile Test Statistics	2

| 2 | ☞ | Execute Manual Tests | 2 days | October 17, 2016 8:00 AM | October 18, 2016 5:00 | ▦ |

Figure C.4 Automatic scheduling

5. Also add one last Manual task *Build Approved* as a milestone. Milestones are significant events with zero duration. For that, after entering all the previous tasks, click in the empty cell. In the **Task** Tab, **Insert** Group select **Milestone** (Diamond shape) and insert details like task name.

Linking Tasks

When you link tasks, you create a relationship between them. MS-Project 2016 supports four types of task relationships (which we have discussed in Chapter 3 of this book). By default, MS-Project 2016 creates finish-to-start links, which means that the first task has to be finished before the second task can start.

To link tasks:

1. In the **Task Name** column, click to select the first task and then hold down the **Ctrl** key, and click to select the remaining tasks. As an alternative, you can select the first and the last tasks, using the **Shift** key, to select all tasks. The order in which the tasks are selected is important. It defines the order in which the tasks are linked.

2. On the **Task** tab of the **Ribbon**, in the **Schedule** group, click the **Link the Selected Tasks** button (Figure C.5). Project 2016 fills in the **Start** and **Finish** fields of the task and links tasks by adding link lines between the task bars in the timescale.

   (You may change the *Finish to Start* relationship which is set by default. For that, double click on the successor task. In the **Task**

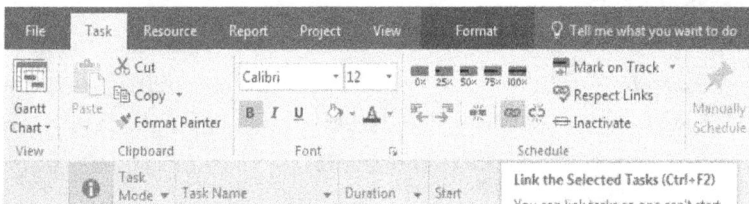

Figure C.5 Linking tasks

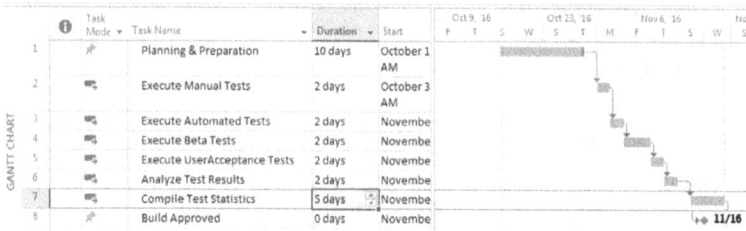

Figure C.6 Start and finish dates do not get adjusted automatically for manually scheduled tasks

Information dialogue that appears select **Predecessors** tab. Next to the predecessor task name, you find the Type as *Finish-to-Start*. Click on the same. You may change the same by selecting a value from the pull down menu there.)

3. Let us see how switching to automatic scheduling will be advantageous as we progress with the planning. For that, change the duration of the *Compile Test Statistics* task to **five days** instead of **two days** (Figure C.6). As you observe the start date of the manually scheduled task, *Build Approved* does not get automatically adjusted and will need to be adjusted manually.

4. Change the duration of the *Build Approved* task back to **two days.**

Inserting a Summary Task

When organizing the tasks for a project, you can group tasks that share characteristics or that will be completed in the same time frame under a summary task. By default, the summary tasks are bold and out-dented, and the subtasks are indented beneath them.

To create a summary task:

1. In the **Task Name** column, select tasks two to five (using **Ctrl** or **Shift** Key).

2. On the **Task** tab of the **Ribbon**, in the **Insert** group, click the *Insert Summary Task* button (see Figure C.7). MS-Project 2016 inserts the new summary task above all the selected tasks, fills in the **Task Name** field with the text **<NewSummaryTask>**, and turns all tasks below it into **subtasks.**

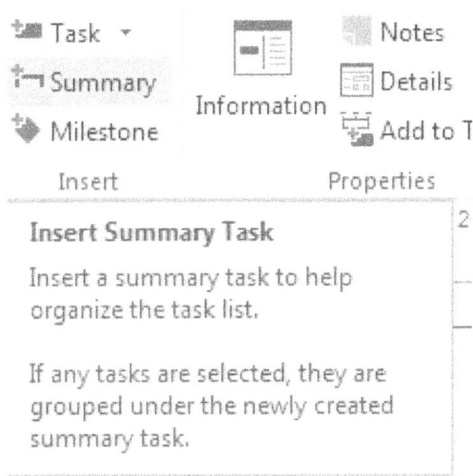

Figure C.7 Inserting summary task

3. Enter *Execute Tests* in the **Task Name** field of the summary task. Another way of creating a summary and sub tasks in a task list is by moving existing tasks a level up or down using outdent-indent buttons. These are there in the Task tab of the ribbon, in the Schedule group (with arrows pointing to left and right sides).

Updating Task Progress

A simple way of tracking task progress is to specify a percentage of completion. You can enter a value between 0 percent (for a task that has not started) and 100 percent (for a task that is finished).

To update a task's percentage of completion:

1. In the **Task Name** column, double-click the *Execute Manual Tests*. The **Task Information** dialog box opens.
2. On the **General** tab, in the **Percent complete** box, enter **50 percent** (see Figure C.8).

   Click the **OK** button. In the timescale, a progress bar is added within the **Execute Manual Tests** task bar which shows the progress on the task (see Figure C.9).

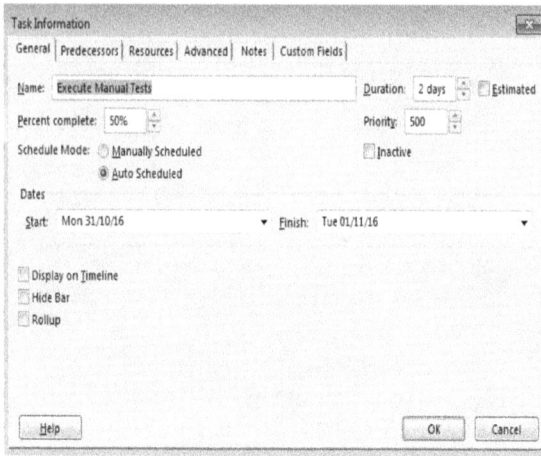

Figure C.8 Entering percentage completion using the task information dialog

Figure C.9 Progress bar displaying the percentage completion

This way, you may set the percentage completion anywhere between 0 and 100 percent. Another quick (yet a limited) way to update is to set the tasks to 0, 25, 50, 75, or 100 percent complete by selecting the tasks in the task table and then clicking the corresponding button in the schedule group on the Task tab of the ribbon (see Figure C.10)

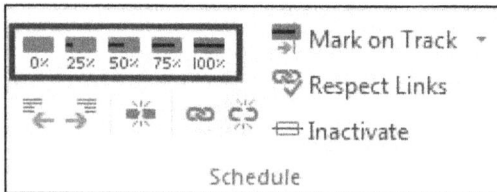

Figure C.10 Updating percentage completion using buttons in the Schedule Group (Task Tab)

Working with Resources

Resources are typically people or material assigned to tasks in a project. People, equipment, or machinery required to accomplish the task are categorized as *Work* resources. Resources can also include materials (like paper, pen drive) or cost (like travel costs, license fees), essential to complete the project.

Adding a Work Resource

You make resources available to assign to tasks within your project, by adding resources in the resource sheet.

To add a work resource:

1. On the **View** tab of the **Ribbon**, in the **Resource Views** group, click the **Resource Sheet** button to switch to the **Resource Sheet** view.
2. In the first row, enter **Project Manager** in the **Resource Name** field (see Figure C.11). Make sure that the **Type** field is set to **Work.** (**P** automatically appears in the **Initials** field).

   You have the option of mentioning a Group Name (like *Managers*) in the Group field while entering the resource information.
3. Enter 20 in the **Std. Rate field.** This sets the hourly rate for that worker to $20.
4. Similarly, add a second resource *QA Engineer* (with Initial **Q),** with a **Std Rate** $10.

ⓘ	Resource Name	Type	Mat Labr	Initials	Group	Max Units	Std. Rate	Ovt Rate	Cost/Use	Accrue At	Base Calendr
1	Project Manager	Work		P		100%	$20.00/hr	$0.00/hr	$0.00	Prorated	Standard

Figure C.11 Entering resource details on the resource sheet

Changing a Resource's Work Hours

By default, a resource's work hours are set to the project's work hours. You can change a resource's work hours to reflect his or her actual work schedule.

Let us change the work hours of *QA Engineer*. To do that:

1. In the **Resource Name** column, double-click the *QA Engineer* resource. The **Resource Information** dialog box opens.

2. On the **General** tab, click the **Change Working Time** button. The **Change Working Time** dialog box pops up.

3. Click the **Work Weeks** tab in the lower section of the dialog box.

4. In the **Name** column, double-click the **[Default]** work week. The **Details for "[Default]" dialog box opens (see Figure C.12).**

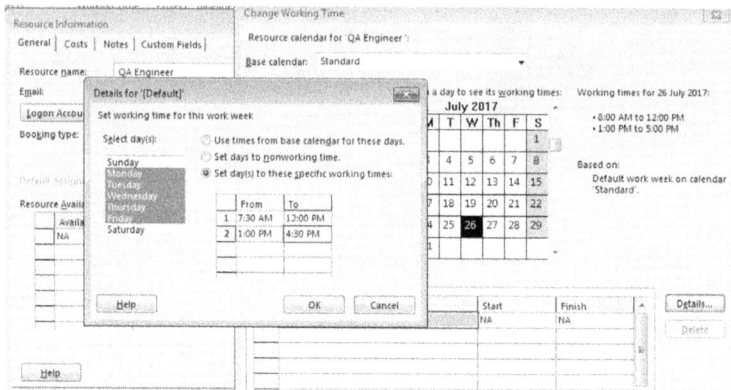

Figure C.12 Changing working time of the resource

1. In the **Select day(s)** box, select Monday through Friday by clicking **Monday**, holding down the **Shift** key, and then clicking **Friday**.

2. Select the **Set day(s) to these specific working times** option.

3. Change the **From** time in the first row to **7:30 AM** and the **To** time in the second row to **4:30 PM**.

4. Click the **OK** button in each dialog box to apply the changes.

On similar lines you can change the project calendar too. To do that, select **Project** Tab on the ribbon and in the **Properties** group, click on the **Change Working Time**. You will get **Change Working Time** dialog, which can be used to define the Project Calendar.

Assigning a Resource to a Task

After you add resources to your project, the next step is to assign them to relevant tasks within your project. There are several ways of doing the same in MS-Project. Let us use one.

To assign a resource to a task:

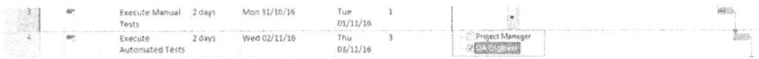

Figure C.13 Assigning a resource using "Resource Names" field

Note: A red person icon may appear in the Indicators field (in the first column) of the task if the resource is overallocated.

1. On the **View** tab of the **Ribbon**, in the **Task Views** group, click the **Gantt Chart** button

    To switch to the **Gantt Chart** view.

2. In the task table, click in the **Resource Names** field of the *Execute Manual Tests* task, click the down arrow that appears, and then select the check-box next to *QA Engineer* to assign him to the task (see Figure C.13). You may recall that we created *QA Engineer*. If you find that the **Resource Names** column is not displayed then use the scroll bar at the bottom of the task table, or move the separator between the Gantt chart area and the task table to display the same.

Assigning Multiple Resources to a task

Some tasks may require multiple resources to complete. However, multiple resources can be assigned to the same task some times, to reduce the amount of time needed to complete the task.

Let us assign multiple resources to an auto scheduled task and see how MS-Project gives you an option of adjusting the amount of the work or the duration. We shall also use the **Assign Resources** dialog box for the same. To assign multiple resources:

1. In the **Task Name** column of the task table, click to select the *Analyze Test Results* task.

2. On the **Resource** tab of the **Ribbon**, in the **Assignments** group, click the **Assign Resources** button. The **Assign Resources** dialog box opens.

3. In the **Resource Name** column, click to select the *QA Engineer* resource, and then click the **Assign** button.

4. Click to select the *Project Manager* resource, and in the **Units** column type 50 (for 50 percent or 0.5 units, indicating that the resource works for half a day), then click the **Assign** button (Figure C.14). Click the **Close** button.

5. Here the task required two work resources to be assigned and this was not done with the intent of just reducing the duration (crashing). Therefore click the exclamation icon that appears to the left of the cell and select the **Increase the amount of work but keep the same duration** option as the reason for assigning work resources to the task (see Figure C.15). A task must be set to **Auto Scheduled** to enable this option.

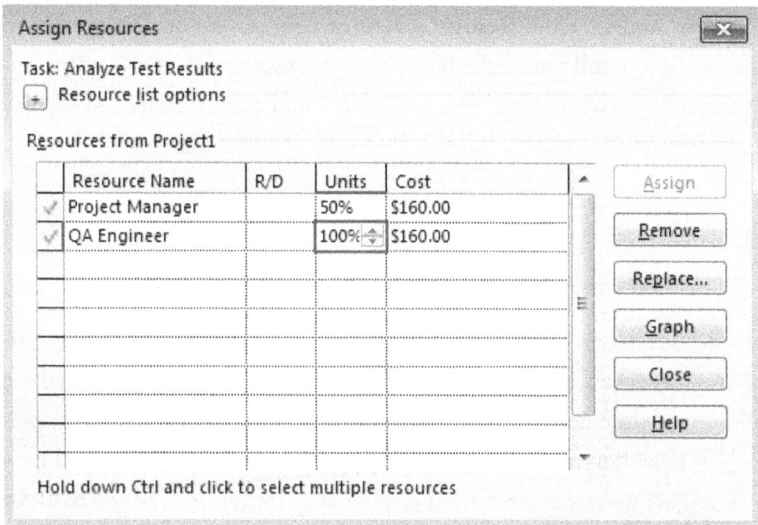

Figure C.14 Assign resources dialog box

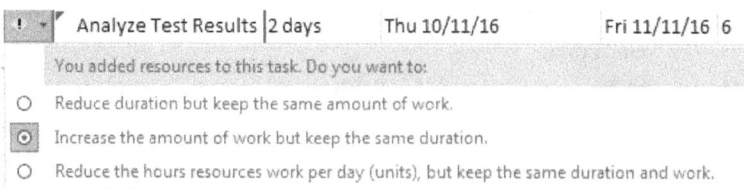

Figure C.15 Click on the exclamation icon and adjust work, resources, or duration

Setting a Scheduling Constraint

We saw how linking tasks can change the start dates of some tasks. We can restrict set on the start or finish date of a task, using constraints. There are several types of constraints that can be placed on a task. By default, *As Soon As Possible* constraint is placed on all tasks.

Let us set *Start No Earlier Than* constraint on a task. To set the scheduling constraint:

1. Make sure that the **Gantt Chart** view is displayed. Select *Compile Test Statistics*.

2. On the **Task** tab of the **Ribbon**, in the **Properties** group, click the **Display Task Details** button. The **Task Details Form** view **displays below** the **Gantt Chart view**. In the **Constraint** section, select **Start No Earlier Than** from the **Constraint list** (see Figure C.16).

   Also set the corresponding constraint **Date** to one day after its original start date.

3. Click the **OK** button. The start and finish dates of the *Compile Test Statistics* task are updated in the task table.

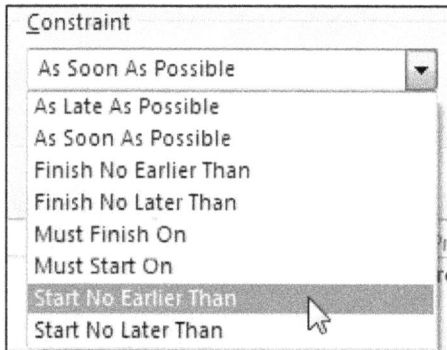

Figure C.16 Constraints list

APPENDIX D

Harnessing MS-Office

We study about creating a project plan with a task list and assigning resources, in detail, in the book. However, in many situations, you may have to share project information like Gantt chart with a colleague, vendor, or a manager, who does not have MS-Project. For example, let us say your supervisor is preparing a presentation and if he or she does not have MS-Project, a slide with Gantt Chart may serve the immediate purpose. Similarly, a colleague may be interested to send a task list created in Microsoft Excel workbook, to help you in planning. If there are hundreds of tasks listed with information like duration, you may be interested in importing task lists directly from other applications like Excel. In this section, we will discuss some such scenarios and how MS-Project can be used with other MS-Office products like Excel and Word.

You can create a graphic-image snapshot of the active view and paste the image into any application that supports graphic images.

Example Problem: Copying Views to Word and PowerPoint

You can create a graphic-image snapshot of the active view and paste the image into an application like MS-Word or PowerPoint that supports graphic images.

You are creating a word document titled **Project-Progress-Report**. In this exercise, you will edit the Word document to communicate the status of a project. You will take the snapshot of Tracking Gantt Chart from the project file **enhancement-complete** and paste it in a document you are preparing. This document can then be shared with your client or supervisor, and they will be able to understand the status of the project, in spite of not having access to MS-Project. To do this:

1. Copy the MS-Word file **Project-Progress-Report.doc** and the project file **enhancement-complete.mpp** in your working directory from **Practice-files/Ap-D**. Open the document **Project-Progress-Report.doc** and take a look. It is a blank document only with the title.

2. Double click and open the file **enhancement-complete.mpp.** You will view the Tracking Gantt Chart related to Software Enhancement as shown in Figure D.1. The Gantt bars for the enhancement summary task and its subtasks are displayed along with percentage completion, and so on.

3. You can view the entire project by selecting the **View** tab and then clicking the **Zoom Entire Project** button from the **Zoom** group. Also, you can move the separating line between the table and the chart, toward left to get a better view of the chart. You need to copy to the progress report (the Word document) the image of the chart visible.

4. In the **Task** tab, **clipboard** group, click on the arrow next to **Copy** button (pull down) to select **Copy Picture.** The **Copy Picture** dialog box appears, which helps you to control the details of the plan you want to copy (Figure D.2). You have the option of saving the image as a GIF (Graphics Interchange Format) file too. The Copy option in the dialog helps you to specify the rows, and the timescale option helps you to specify time period for copying select portion of the plan. Accept the default options and click **OK.** Project copies a graphic image of the Gantt Chart for just the selected rows to the Windows Clipboard.

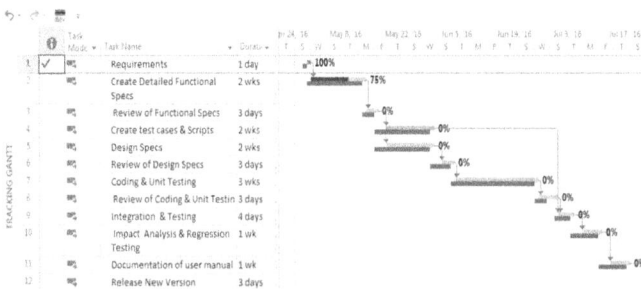

Figure D.1 Tracking Gantt view of the project, which needs to be copied

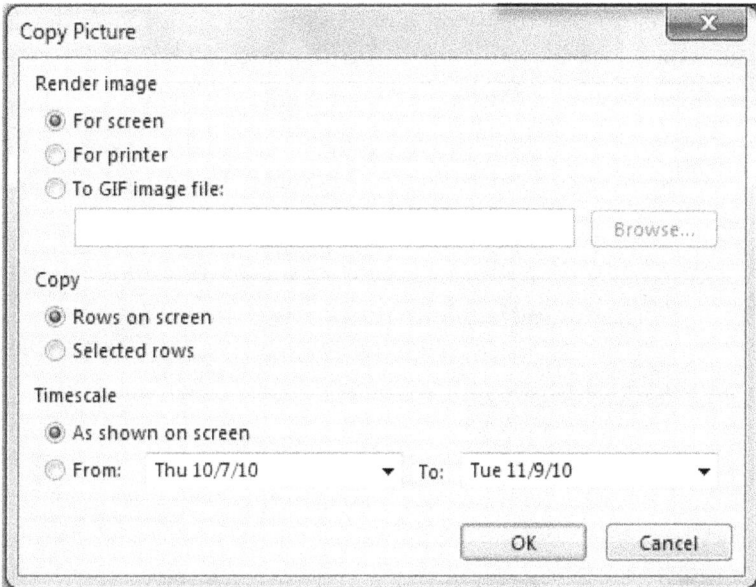

Figure D.2 Copy Picture dialog with different options

5. As a last step you have to paste this image in the MS-Word document, **Project-Progress-Report.doc** that you had opened. Click on the document and place the cursor suitably below the title *PROJECT PROGRESS REPORT*. Using **Ctrl + V** or contextual menu (available on right click), paste the image (Figure D.3). **Save** the Word file and close both files (the Project and the Word files).

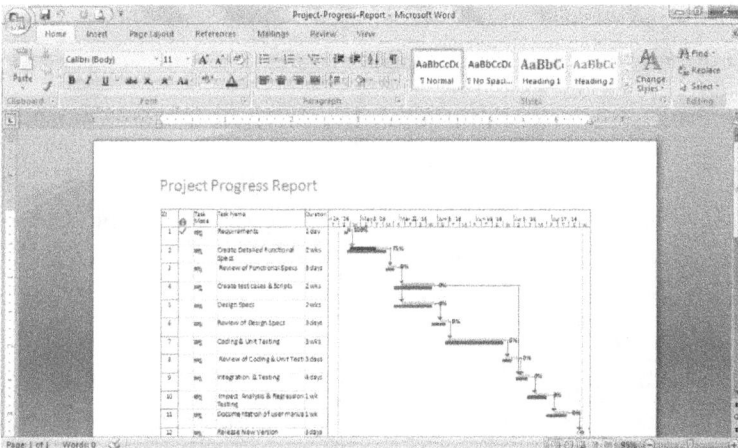

Figure D.3 Snapshot of the active view has been copied in the word file

You can quickly copy most views and reports from MS-Project to paste into e-mail messages and PowerPoint presentations. Some views like Team Planner and Resource Form cannot be directly copied from MS-Project . You may use a screen capture utility (or Print Screen button on your keyboard), if you need a visual snapshot of a view or report that cannot be directly copied from MS-Project.

Example Problem: Importing Task List from MS-Office Excel

Let us say a colleague in your company has sent you an Excel work-book that contains her or his recommended tasks and durations of activities for some work related to mobile application development. You would like to import these data into MS-Project and create a Gantt Chart.

When saving data to or opening data from other formats, Project uses maps (also called *import/export maps* or *data-maps*) to transfer information from data file of one program to data file of another program. You use data maps to specify which individual fields in the source data file correspond to which individual fields in the destination data file. Once you set up an import/export map, you can use it over and over again, if required. When you have large number of files to be imported, saving the map with a suitable name can be of help.

You change the trust center settings, set up an import/export map, and then transfer task list–related data.

1. Copy the **AppDevelopment.xls** file to your working directory from **Practice-files/Ap-D**. This is an Excel workbook. If you have Excel installed on your computer, open the workbook (Figure D.4). This is a file you will import into Project. Observe the names and order of the columns (field names), the presence of a header row (the labels at the top of the columns), in the work-sheet named *Task_Table1*. Close the workbook file without saving the changes. Although this step is not a must, it helps in mapping fields.

Figure D.4 Task sheet in the Excel workbook

2. You may not be able to open files of MS-Office applications like MS Excel and files from legacy MS-Project files in Project 2016 because of security settings. You have to change this setting to start the import. (You may restore it to its original setting, if required, once you are done with the import). To do that in MS-Project, on the **File** tab, click **Options**. The Project Options dialog box appears. Click **Trust Center** (on the left-hand side) as shown in Figure D.5. Click the **Trust Center Settings** button to open the Trust Center dialog box. Click **Legacy Formats**. Under **Legacy Formats**, select radio button **Prompt when loading files with legacy or nondefault file format**

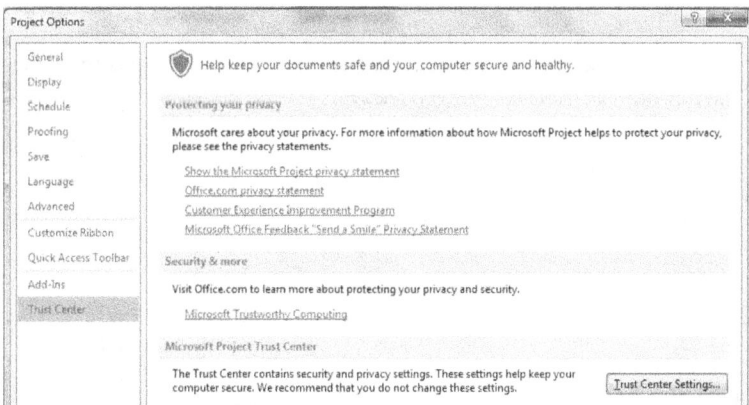

Figure D.5 Use the Project Options dialog to change the trust center–related settings

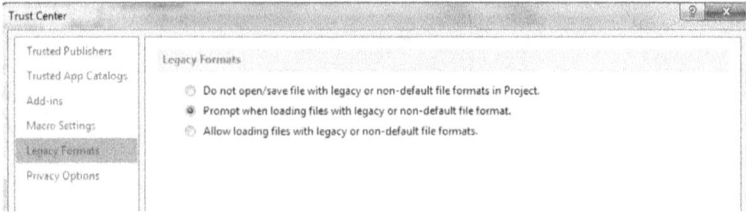

Figure D.6 Allow Legacy formats to open in MS-Project interactively, at the trust center

(Figure D.6). Click **OK** to close the **Trust Center** dialog box, and then click **OK** again to close the **Project Options** dialog box.

3. With these changes in settings, now you are ready to import an Excel workbook. Click the **File** tab, then click **New** and **New from Excel Workbook** as shown in Figure D.**7**. Navigate to your working folder. In the file type box (initially labeled **Projects**), select **Excel Workbook** as shown in Figure D.8. To understand what all file formats can be imported in MS-Project just scroll through the file type box.

Select the **AppDevelopment** file, and then click **Open**. The Import Wizard appears as shown in Figure D.9. This wizard helps you import structured data from a different format to Project.

4. Click **Next**. The second page of the Import Wizard appears.

The Import Wizard uses maps to organize the way that structured data from another file format is imported into MS-Project. For this exercise, you will create a new map. Ensure that **New map** is selected, and then click **Next**. The Import Mode page of the Import Wizard appears. Make sure that **As a new project** is selected, and then click

Figure D.7 Start creating a new project using Excel workbook

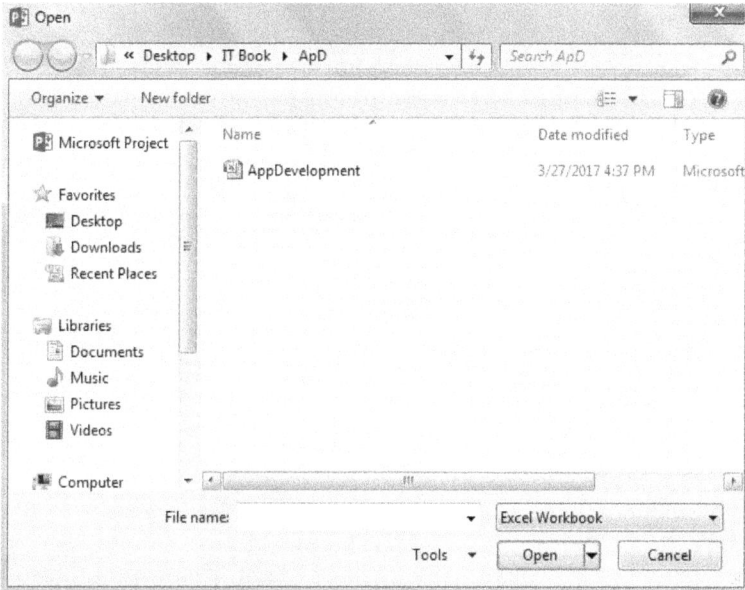

Figure D.8 Select appropriate Excel workbook format in the file type box

Next. The Map Options page of the Import Wizard appears. Select the **Tasks** check-box, and make ensure that **Import includes headers** (column headings) is selected too.

5. Click **Next**.

The Task Mapping page of the Import Wizard appears (Figure D.10). Here, you identify the source worksheet within the Excel workbook and specify how you want to map the data from the source worksheet to Project fields. In the **Source worksheet name** box, select **Task_Table 1**.

Task_Table 1 is the name of the sheet in the Excel workbook. Project analyzes the header row names from the worksheet and suggests the Project field names that are probable matches. You could change the mapping to other fields optionally over here.

6. Click **Next**.

The last page of the Import Wizard appears. Here, you have the option of saving the settings for the new import map, which is useful when you anticipate importing similar data into MS-Project later on. You can skip this step over here, as you have only one file this time around.

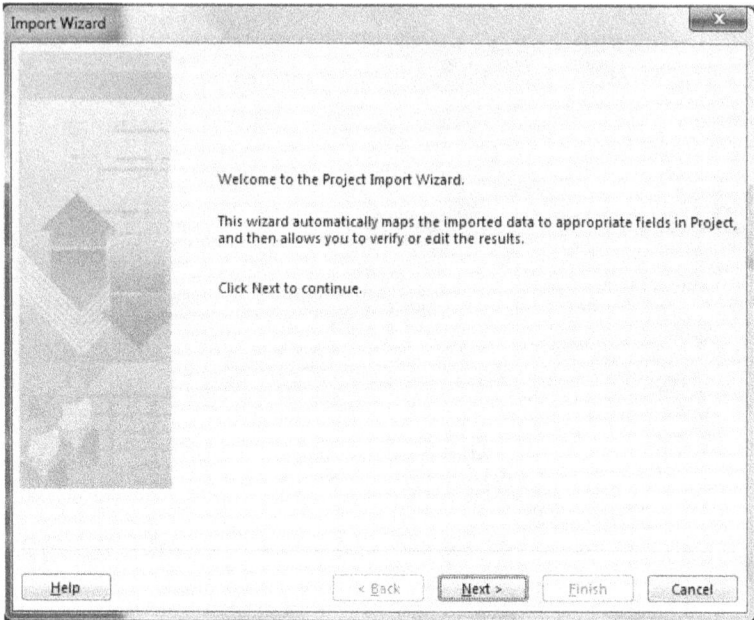

Figure D.9 Project import wizard helps to map the data in an intuitive and interactive manner

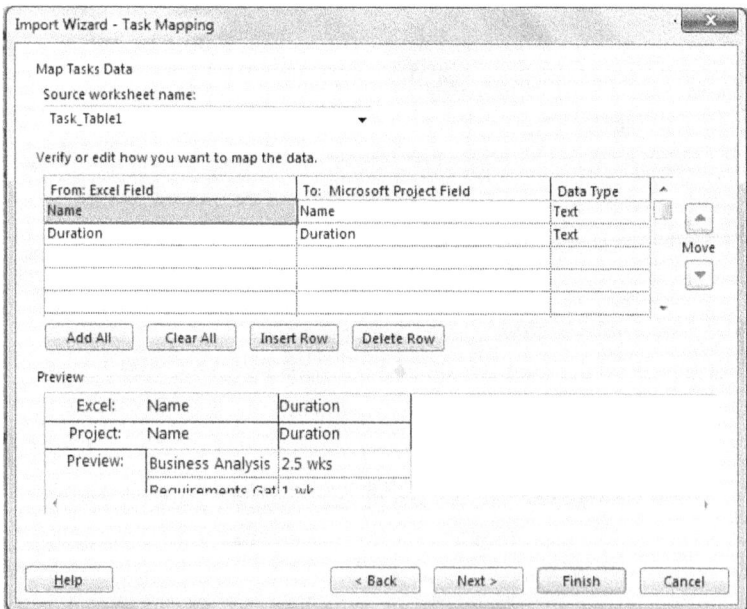

Figure D.10 Map the task information appropriately to relevant fields of MS-Project

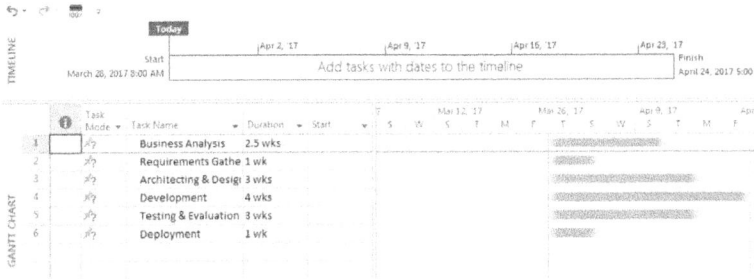

Figure D.11 Imported task list for the bridge project

Click **Finish**. Project imports the Excel data into a new plan. You will get a manually scheduled task list (unless you had changed the settings to automatic tasks) with the current date as the project start date in MS-Project as shown in Figure D.11. You may link the tasks, create resources, and further develop the plan in MS-Project.

Note

1. A simple task list with only Task names and duration is used to demonstrate the feature. However, one can import more complex data, with many fields like Start Date and Finish Date from Excel into MS-Project.
2. It is also possible (on similar lines) to transfer the resources and assignments data to Excel workbook, using the export feature of MS-Project.

Getting Help for MS-Project

Often you may need informal product support and a way to broaden your expertise of using MS-Project. There are many user groups that are active online. Some of these conduct events and meet locally too. You may be able to share tips and tricks with other users by being a part of these. The following are a few groups that may be of interest to you.

- *MPUG* stands for the Microsoft Project Users Group. It provides articles, webinars, discussion groups, and career opportunities. You may visit www.mpug.com for more information.
- Official site of Microsoft Products using the link products. office.com and then navigate to the *Project* link given at the bottom. Another useful link that provides links to discussion groups, and so on, is technet.microsoft.com
- Folks associated with the Microsoft Most Valuable Professional (MVP) program can be of help to you. You may visit project.mvps.org for more information. There are links to blogs, question–answers, and third-party software on the site.
- You may also become a member of the LinkedIn groups like *Microsoft Certified Trainers* and *Microsoft Project Users* and participate in the discussion.

Understanding the Project Server

Before discussing about the server let us look at the definitions of two important terms, namely program management and portfolio management. *Program management* is the process of *managing* several related projects together with the intention of improving an organization's performance. Portfolio is a collection of programs, projects, and/or operations managed as a group. The components of a portfolio may not necessarily be interdependent or even related—but they are managed together as a group to achieve strategic objectives.

Now let us understand the functions of the Project Server in brief. Tools like Project Standard and Project Professional (in stand-alone mode) can help you to manage project from a stand-alone machine. You can do project planning, create tasks and sub tasks, assign those tasks to resources, track those tasks, and generate reports with these. However, it is not easy to manage multiple mega projects in a big organization, with hundreds of planners and managers. In an enterprise like that you need to use a server. Project Server is Microsoft's Project Management software that allows one to do project management, portfolio management, program management work management, and related things for an organization.

Project Server is a multi tiered system built on SharePoint architecture as shown in Figure F.1. Project Server is made up of a server component (the "server" software) that can be accessed and operated from clients. The client can be a desktop application like Project Professional (about which we have discussed in the book) or Project Web App (PWA) browser–based software or a customized (proprietary or third party) app as shown in Figure F.1. Project Server 2016 runs as a service application

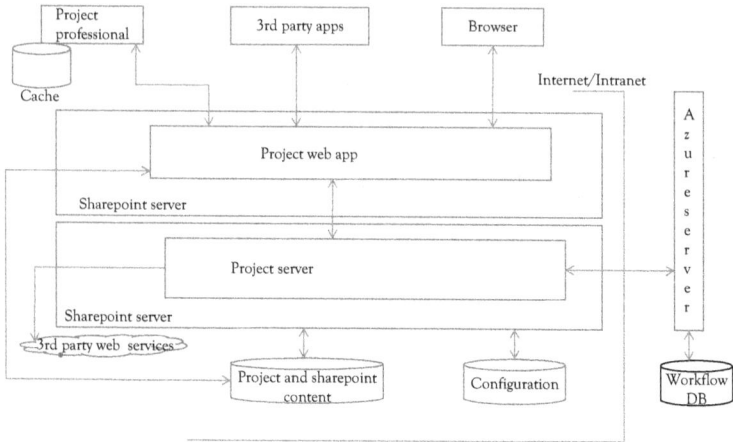

Figure F.1 Project server architecture

in SharePoint Server 2016 Enterprise. In SharePoint 2016, Project Server is integrated into the platform making the deployment easier.

PWA is the browser-based interface to Project Server that project managers and team members can use. PWA can be used to manage Project Professional plans (MPP files), SharePoint task lists, and plans created directly in PWA.

APPENDIX G
Keyboard Shortcuts

Keyboard shortcuts are supported throughout MS-Project. To see the keyboard shortcuts for the available commands, press the **Alt** key (Figure G.1). Once you start using the keyboard shortcuts to access the tabs, the next level of keyboard shortcuts appear for other submenus. For example, if you select "U" for the resource tab, you will find that you may use "G" to get Assign Resources dialog. Continue pressing letters until you press the letter of the command or control that you want to use. In some cases, you must first press the letter of the group that contains the command. To cancel the action that you are taking and hide the Key-Tips, press **Alt**.

Other keyboard shortcuts, such as Save file (Ctrl + S), are generally available at all times. Table G.1 gives a select list of such commonly used keystrokes, although it is not a complete one. For keyboard shortcuts in which you press two or more keys at the same time, the keys to press are separated by a plus sign (+) in MS-Project 2016 Help.

Figure G.1 Key stroke shortcuts are displayed with the Alt key

Table G.1 Some useful commonly used keyboard shortcuts

To do this	Press
Save project file	\<Ctrl\> + \<S\>
Close current project	\<Ctrl\> + \<W\>
Open existing project in the backstage view	\<Ctrl\> + \<O\>
Open a project file (display the Open dialog box)	\<Ctrl\> + F12

Print/Print preview	\<Ctrl\> + \<P\>
Task or resource information	\<Shift\> + \<F2\>
Go to selected task	\<Ctrl\> + \<Shift\> + \<F5\>
Link selected task	\<Ctrl\> + \<F2\>
Unlink selected task	\<Ctrl\> + \<Shift\> + F2
Create a hyperlink	\<Ctrl\> + \<K\>
Zoom out	\<Ctrl\> + \<Shift\> + \< * \>
Zoom in	\<Ctrl\> + \</\>
Copy a picture of the screen to the clipboard	Print Screen
Copy a picture of the selected window to the clipboard	Alt + Print Screen
Undo	\<Ctrl\> + \<Z\>
Redo	\<Ctrl\> + \<Y\>

References

Chau, L.H. 2007. *ACE Engineering Practice Tutorial 2- MS Project 2007.* Published on website xa.yimg.com (Adapted).

Samant, U.M. n.d. *MS-Project 2007 and PMBOK, 2010, Tutorial of MGBS Consulting.* Troy, Michigan, USA (Adapted).

About the Author

Ulhas M. Samant is founder and director of PM-Skills, a project management training and consultancy firm, from Pune, India. He has extensive experience in managing projects related to information technology and engineering and has worked in companies like Bajaj Auto, Tata Motors, and Patni Computer Systems (later merged with Capgemini). He is a graduate with M. Tech from NIT, Warangal, India. He has offered project scheduling consultancy for companies like Crompton Greaves and Juniper Networks. He is also the author of another book titled "Computer support for successful project management: using MS-project 2016 with construction projects." He blogs regularly about MS-Project and project management at pmmantra.blogspot.in

Index

Task types, 36–38
TCPI. *See* To complete performance
    index
Test execution task, 36–37
To complete performance index
    (TCPI), 62

Waterfall model
  coding, 4
  requirement analysis and definition,
    3–4
  software design, 4

software integration and
    verification, 4
system design, 4
system validation, 4–5
WBS. *See* Work breaksown structure
Work breaksown structure (WBS)
  codes for task list in project,
    16–20
  creating, 13–15
  dictionary, 15–16
  numbering, 15–16
  resources, 20